BOOKS IN THIS SERIES

1. **THE DIARY OF AMOS LEE**
   I Sit, I Write, I Flush!

2. **THE DIARY OF AMOS LEE**
   Girls, Guts and Glory!

3. **THE DIARY OF AMOS LEE**
   I'm Twelve, I'm Tough, I Tweet!

THE DIARY OF AMOS LEE
I'm Twelve, I'm Tough, I Tweet!

Written by
ADELINE FOO

Illustrated by
STEPHANIE WONG

FIFTH PRINTING, 2011
Text © Adeline Foo 2010
Illustrations © Epigram 2010

PUBLISHED BY EPIGRAM
1008 Toa Payoh North #03-08 Singapore 318996
Tel: (65) 6292 4456/ Fax: (65) 6292 4414
enquiry@epigram.com.sg / www.epigram.com.sg

DISTRIBUTED BY
Market Asia Distributors
601 Sims Drive #04-05
Pan-I Complex, Singapore 387382
Tel: (65) 6744 8483, 6744 8486
jl@marketasia.com.sg

ILLUSTRATIONS AND COVER DESIGN BY
Stephanie Wong

EDITED BY
Ruth Wan

NATIONAL LIBRARY BOARD SINGAPORE CATALOGUING IN PUBLICATION DATA
Foo, Adeline, 1971-
The Diary of Amos Lee: I'm Twelve, I'm Tough, I Tweet! / Written by Adeline Foo,
Illustrated by Stephanie Wong. – Singapore: Epigram, 2010.
p. cm.
ISBN-13: 978-981-08-7132-1 (pbk.)

1. Boys – Singapore – Diaries – Juvenile fiction. 2. Blogs – Juvenile fiction.
3. Competition (Psychology) – Juvenile fiction. I. Wong, Stephanie, 1979- II. Title.

PZ7
S823 – dc22 OCN668143916

ALL RIGHTS RESERVED.
No part of this book may be reproduced
without prior consent from the publisher.

Printed in Singapore.

I'm sooooo looking forward to completing my last year in primary school!

Last year, my swim team came in first in the inter-school relay competition and I won an award for a science magazine that I wrote.

This year, the school is introducing a Tween Idol popularity contest. Aaawwww, they must have had me in mind when they thought of this.

I did something to check how popular I am. I started a Twitter page, and at the last check, I've already chalked up a decent list of followers!

Man... the power of the Internet. Although I was away on a family holiday, I was able to keep in touch with my best friends, Alvin and Anthony, and check on the number of followers I have on Twitter. My friends prefer using Facebook. But that's something Mum says I've to wait till next year to sign up for, when I'm 13.

Mum has been philosophical lately. Last night, she said, "With fame comes responsibility." Actually, it should be, "With great power comes great responsibility." I didn't think Peter Parker's uncle was a wise man, but that's not important. Mum's right. I should put my great fame to good use. My new year resolution is to brainwash my Twitter followers. I must get them to vote for me to be Tween Idol. I MUST win! I will not leave school without being remembered.

Famous Amos. The 1st Tween Idol. This is it. The trophy is mine. I'll just have to be less blatant about wanting it, or it may inspire copycats to compete with me. Like Michael, my arch enemy. Bet he doesn't realise how popular I am. 27 followers! Eat that, twit!

I'm sooooo looking forward to starting the new school year!

Monday, 4 January

BACK TO SCHOOL

It was great seeing everyone in school. Alvin and Anthony were surprised when I told them I had been "working" for Coach during the school holidays. He was asked by the principal to start an online magazine. Guess who he called for help? Poor me!

Fat good it did for my ego. No one read it! I knew because when I asked around, NOT A SINGLE PERSON remembered receiving a copy of it via email. Sheesh... My two best friends weren't even interested to hear what I had written for the magazine.

But when I showed them my new iPhone, they couldn't stop asking questions. Alvin was really intrigued with one of the apps. It allows me to rate my poop, from colour to consistency. Mum doesn't know about this of course. Alvin laughed really hard when I showed him my achievement last night.

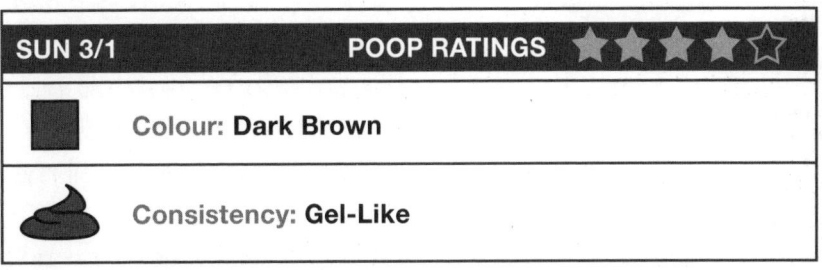

He asked me what I ate. I told him I had french fries dipped in chilli and ice cream.

Thursday, 7 January

TWITTER CHECK

What's happening?   140

Latest: Greetings from the Loo.   **Tweet**

Famous Amos
2 tweets

5 Following   **27** Followers   **0** Listed

Number of followers: 27
I looked at Justin Bieber's Twitter page. He has 2.8 million followers! Oh man... I need to do something about this. Even if I'm only aiming for 0.00000000001 per cent of his fame, I should have something more to show.

Friday, 8 January

MICHAEL

I saw him during swimming practice. He looks bigger and tougher. Just what does he eat? Some idiot told me that Michael is on Facebook. Why did he have to tell me how many friends he has? 453! How did he get so many friends? Sheeesh... what did he do? Get his entire flat of neighbours to add him as a friend?

Monday, 11 January

TWITTER CHECK

Number of followers: 31
Ah ha! I have four new followers. Hooray!

Tuesday, 12 January

POOP TWEET

Wednesday, 13 January

A PROMISE

Mum assured me that she won't be reading my diary anymore. Right, Mum! I'm almost 12 and I deserve respect and privacy! But she said she will be following my tweets. I can live with that.

Friday, 15 January

WRITING FOR THE SCHOOL MAGAZINE

Coach asked if I wanted to continue writing for the online magazine. I took the opportunity to ask why he picked me. He said I was the only writer he could find, and added that since I had won an award last year for my Science magazine, I shouldn't let my talent go to waste.

Really, he has no clue that inspiration doesn't strike easily for a writer. I have to thank my cat, Tom, for that award! I had written about him swallowing a lizard whole - head, body, four legs and one wriggly tail. I likened his killer instinct to finding the drive to excel in swimming, to "kill and win"!

I suggested to Coach that we give the online magazine a sassy title, something like "Poop Fiction" to get kids excited about reading. That was when he laughed and said he loved toilet humour. But actually, I was only trying to be a smart-mouth. And when I said, "The daily scoop on poop rhymes," he really cracked up. Boy, this is one funny Coach.

Poop Fiction by Amos Lee.

I'm such a genius!

Saturday, 16 January

POOP FICTION

Coach gave me a list of guidelines to follow.
He suggested writing about:

1. **History**
   (Boring! Hmmm... maybe I could write about the history of the toilet. That would be really funny!)

2. **Useful information**
   (Right. Like poop trivia people didn't know about.)

3. **Funny stuff**
   (Ha! I'm sure he means funny and disgusting.)

4. **Must be inspired by things that we take for granted**
   (Right. Like toilet paper? Got it!)

Starting on my research right away. Guess Coach wouldn't mind if I skip swimming practice for the next two weeks! I'm serious about this job. I'm such a good and responsible boy, ha!

Friday, 29 January

FINAL DRAFT

I took two whole weeks to do my research! I couldn't do anything else until I had finished. I used the Internet and visited the public library. I even checked out many encyclopaedias. Man, it was really hard work. But it was fun. I must be the only boy who dutifully reported for "work" at the library. There I was, still dressed in uniform after school, poring over any book that had the word "toilet" in its title. I read everything! Finally, I finished my article. I read it over and over again. I even did several spell checks on the computer. Now I can email it out. Blast it off into cyberspace!

FEATURE #1

POOP FICTION

A SCOOP ON POOP!

Let's celebrate the first issue of Poop Fiction by giving thanks for the greatest invention of humankind! The toilet. Did you know that we owe the invention of the modern day toilet to Sir John Harrington, an Englishman who invented the world's first flushing toilet in 1596? But what was life like before the toilet was invented?

A long time ago, about 10,000 years back, people did their big business anywhere it pleased them. Archaeologists have found the earliest evidence of pipes built to carry human waste in Scotland. In the areas we know as Pakistan and Syria today, there is also evidence of ancient people who had used pipes and water to get rid of human waste. But more concrete evidence of bathroom invention was found on the island of Crete, which historians have labelled as the birthplace of European civilisation, around 2,000 B.C.. Palaces that were built had more than 1,500 rooms, and they included bathrooms with toilets, built with comfy wooden seats flushed by rainwater.

Around 500 B.C., the Romans had public toilets where men could sit and chat while engaging in big business. Bottoms were cleaned with a sponge on a stick, kept in a pail of water mixed with salt. Yucks! Remember, toilet paper was not invented yet. The Romans used a sponge on a stick to wipe their bottoms clean. Now the question that begs to be answered is, did everyone share just one stick?

In other parts of Europe, in medieval times, people threw waste out their windows! The streets were convenient dumping grounds, and walking the streets meant you had to watch out or you could get hit by human waste! Imagine the awful smell! The chamber pot was used for conducting big business, and when it was emptied out the window, you were supposed to shout, "Gardez l'eau!" That's French for, "Watch out for the water!"

Kings and Dukes who lived in castles would relieve themselves in a little room built in the castle wall. Called the garderobe, it meant a "wardrobe" where one would sit on a cold stone seat, and whatever was released from the bottom would drop into the moat surrounding the castle! This explained why the moat was an effective deterrent for invading enemies. Imagine having to swim across the moat in excrement to scale the castle wall. Gross!

Now let's get back to Sir John Harrington. He invented the first flushing toilet for Queen Elizabeth I. He called his toilet "Ajax", and built it with a valve that would release water from a water closet when pulled. This would flush the toilet. But Ajax never became popular with the masses. It was probably too expensive to be installed. It was only around the 1880s that the toilet became popular. At that time, Thomas Crapper, an English plumber, made it "popular" by selling it affordably to ordinary people. (Sir) John, Crap(per)... hmmm, now we know the origins of these names which have been associated with the toilet.

We refer to sitting on the toilet bowl as "sitting on the throne". Why? Well, we owe the "throne" to King Louis XIV of France, who had a special throne he sat on at night. It was called a closestool where he would relieve himself! The King was also a multi-tasker. While holding court on his "throne", he would write letters and issue orders! (So I can't claim to be the first to write my diary in the toilet. King Louis wrote while sitting on the potty way before me!) It was recorded that at the King's most vulnerable moments, the lords would ask for grants of money or special favours. Doesn't a king deserve his privacy? Sheesh...

The toilets of today are so vastly different, depending on which part of the world you're living in. Some have you sit, some prefer that you squat. There are flushing toilets with built-in water-saving features that control the amount of water used. There are bidets invented by the French to wash your bums. But surely, the ultra-modern toilet award must go to the Japanese! For they've invented toilets that can do almost anything. Spray-clean your bum, air-dry it, deodorise smells, and even warm the toilet seat! Need we ask for better comfort?

If I were to ask, "What do you have in common with famous people?", what would you say? Think of pop idols like Justin Bieber and Miley Cyrus (Hannah Montana), or even President Obama, the American President. Well, when the urge strikes and your bowels crank up, you need the toilet. So whether we're 12, 42, or 101, when we need to do big business, regardless of whether we're famous, rich or poor, we're all equal, perching on the toilet bowl!

Look out for my next feature, when I will discuss the invention of toilet paper. In the meantime, enjoy the scoop, aaaannnd... bombs away!

amos lee

Amos Lee for Poop Fiction

Monday, 1 February

TWITTER CHECK

OH MY GOODNESS! How did this happen? It's a miracle! I have 425 followers now! I asked Mum if her friends had anything to do with it. She said no. But she was very happy for me.

Tuesday, 2 February

THE MYSTERY SOLVED

Many of my classmates came up to me to congratulate me today. They had read Poop Fiction and enjoyed it. Well, that explains the phenomenal jump in my number of followers. They are all my readers!

Thursday, 4 February

POOP TWEET

Friday, 5 February

MY SISTER, MISS WHINY-PESKY -AND-IRRITATING

WPI said it was cool that her brother is so famous in school. She told Mum proudly that she saw all her friends reading Poop Fiction in the school toilet. Man... why would I want to know this? Last year, I could tolerate her better as I hardly saw her. She was in school in the afternoon when I got home from school. Just my luck that she is in the morning session this year with me. I heard her tell Mum that she wants to be famous like me. Pleaaaassssee! There can only be one celebrity in the family, ha!

Monday, 8 February

MICHAEL AGAIN

Anthony told me that Michael has posted lots of pictures of himself on Facebook. He posed topless and wore different swimming briefs. Humph! What a lame excuse to get more friends. I can just imagine what he put under his profile. "Michael, the Olympic dream. Everyone's my friend!"

Wednesday, 10 February

FAN MAIL

Something weird is happening. The admin clerk from the principal's office passed me 22 letters that were addressed to me. They were all anonymous. And guess what?

Whooohoooo! I'm famous. I'm famous. I'm Mr Popular... oh yeah. 21 letters were written by readers that said they really enjoyed reading my article "A Scoop on Poop!" But one letter said I was irrelevant. Whatever that means. But I was curious, so I asked Mum. She said the right word should be "irreverent", which means, disrespectful.

Who, me? Pleaaaassseee...! One hate mail out of 22 letters will not dampen my fame.

Saturday, 13 February

MUM WANTS TO WRITE AGAIN

Mum said she was so inspired by my tweets and articles that she has decided to get back to writing. She had quit her job to take care of us, but if she's getting back to work, who's going to take care of Everest, my baby brother? Not me, for sure! Mum said she will stick to blogging from home. It's more flexible than finding a writing job outside. She said that when she has created a huge fan base, she will be able to attract advertisers to her blog. Wow! I hadn't realised that you can make money from blogging! It's useful to know that. I could do with a famous Mum. Another thing to add to my popularity. Oh yeah...

Monday, 15 February

POOP TWEET

Wow! People do follow my tweets!

Thanks for the tissue paper, bro!

Wednesday, 17 February

AMOS HARD AT WORK

It took less time to do the research for my second article. I'm getting really good! It's also exciting uncovering trivia I wouldn't normally have read. Hmmm... maybe I could make a career out of writing! I took only one week to complete my second article. It also feels great to hear Coach say I'm doing a great job with Poop Fiction.

Tuesday, 23 February

LESS SWIMMING, MORE WRITING!

I spoke to Coach about cutting back on swimming practice to give me more time to write for Poop Fiction. He looked reluctant. But when I hinted that he would get into the principal's good books for producing a popular school magazine, he beamed and nodded his head eagerly. Yeah! I've got Coach on a leash. Boy, am I good or what.

FEATURE #2

POOP FICTION

THE MANY FACES OF THE HUMBLE TOILET PAPER

Before toilet paper was invented, people had to resort to creative means to wipe their bottoms. Empty coconut shells, grass, straw, snow, moss, and even sand! Rich people used wool or lace. The poor, if they couldn't get hold of anything, used their bare hands.

When paper was invented, it made toilet-going somewhat easier. Newspapers and telephone directories found new meaning as recycled paper! But it was only in 1857 that the first commercial toilet paper was produced. Joseph Gayetty, an American businessman, printed and sold individual sheets of toilet paper with his name on them. Toilet paper is such a basic need that we take for granted. I'm amazed that it took 260 years after the invention of the first flush toilet for people to realise that they need not depend on nature or their hands to clean their bums.

These days, people take their toilet paper very seriously. In America for example, consumers spend more than US$3.7 billion a year buying toilet paper! Commercial manufacturers of toilet paper spend millions of dollars on TV, web and print ads to sell their products. Innovative programmes have included setting up restrooms in the middle of New York City's Times Square to let consumers try different brands of toilet paper! Talk about "creative sampling", huh!

So how much toilet paper is used by the average consumer? Data in America has shown that an average of 20,805 sheets of toilet paper are used per person each year. At an average length of 11.3 cm per sheet to wipe your backside, that's close to 2,351 metres of toilet paper used by the average person every year! (That's, incidentally, the height of FIVE Empire State Buildings!) Sure is a lot of toilet paper to get rid of human waste...

So do you agree that these companies are justified in spending millions to ensure that our "bottoms receive the best"?

Amos Lee

Amos Lee for Poop Fiction

The Editor of Poop Fiction *(er.., that would be the swimming coach)* has decided that readers who bother to write in with their comments after reading Poop Fiction will receive rewards. But he said he will not accept anonymous letters. Please state your name and class.

Here are two questions to start you off:
1. Do you stand or sit when you clean your bottom?
   (Amos Lee's question)
2. What creative uses of toilet paper can you think of?
   (The Editor's question)

Monday, 1 March

MICHAEL, A JEALOUS SOUL

Fame invites trouble. Michael has been bad-mouthing me during swimming practice. I wasn't there but I heard it from both Alvin and Anthony. He has started a petition on Facebook to ban Poop Fiction. He says it's disgusting and makes a mockery of reading. What does he know? Has he even read my magazine? It's so well written. It's funny. And it's irreverent! He may be the top student in school, but he can't blame me if I got invited to write for the school magazine instead! Sheesh....

Thursday, 4 March

MUM'S BLOG

Horror of horrors! My mum is blogging about ALL MY FAMILY SECRETS! This is really, really bad. I peeped at her laptop when she took Everest to the paediatrician. Her blog tracks her life starting from giving birth to me till now. The most damaging entry was this one:

Of all my three children, Amos wins the "Best Milk Guzzler" award. He was so hungry all the time! I breastfed him till he was a big baby, almost 17 months old. He could walk and run, but he still needed breast milk before he could fall asleep.

This spells the end of my fame! What will happen when my enemies chance upon my mum's blog? Oh man... the trouble I'm in. Best Milk Guzzler Award? Yucks! Disgusting!

Monday, 8 March

TWITTER CHECK

What's happening? 60

Latest: Look out for the 2nd Issue of Poop Fiction, OUT NOW!

Tweet

Famous Amos
15 tweets

15 Following **513** Followers **15** Listed

Number of followers: 513
This is fantastic! I wonder how many friends Michael has.

Wednesday, 10 March

MICHAEL'S FB FRIENDS

Alvin said Michael has added him as a friend. Anthony confessed he has become Michael's friend too. It seems that everyone is now Michael's friend! Even Somaly, Alvin's girlfriend, and the other girls in class. I feel so sick. Alvin said Michael has 574 friends now. Oh man... I'm still behind him. And he doesn't even need to do anything! I have to spend so much time doing research for Poop Fiction!

Friday, 12 March

A POPULARITY CONTEST

The principal finally made the announcement about the Tween Idol popularity contest.

There had been so many rumours going around. The contest is in search of a community role model that inspires excellence in others.

Yeah! That sounds like me! I'm so excited! This is a great way to leave school, by winning the FIRST TWEEN IDOL AWARD. I'm so happy. It's mine. It's mine. It's mine. Amos Lee, the Tween Idol!

Tuesday, 16 March

TO BE IMMORTALISED

Everyone has been talking about the Tween Idol popularity contest the last few days. I'm soooooo looking forward to getting in AND becoming FAMOUS when I win it! I heard WPI telling Mum about the contest. She said she's jealous of both me and Everest, our baby brother, for having famous names.

Really, what's she jealous about? Is it a claim to immortality to be named after cookies? And does she think Everest will be thrilled to know he's named after a mountain? There's no way my brother can ever match the feat of the Singapore Women Everest Team, in scaling Mount Everest last year. To be named after a mountain to commemorate their special achievement - pleeeuuuuzzzz! Only my mother is capable of thinking of that.

Everest sure can't climb a mountain but he's a champion crawler. I can see him putting the remote control in his mouth. Muuuuuuuuuummmmmmmmmmmmmmmmm!

Friday, 19 March

MICHAEL PHUI THE DOLPHIN

I heard Michael has been clocking in slightly under two minutes for his 200 metres butterfly stroke swimming timing. Oh man... that's VERY FAST! I can imagine the impact he's creating. No one, not even Alvin, can swim that fast! Hmmm... I have a bad feeling about this. Maybe he thinks by swimming so fast, he can win more friends?

Tuesday, 23 March

TRYING TO STAY IN THE LEAD OF THE RACE

Coach cautioned me about spending too much time on Poop Fiction. Really! What does he know? I need to work harder to win more followers! Everyone loves a winner! Michael is now so popular because of his swimming prowess. Poop Fiction is my only chance to get ahead of him!

Friday, 26 March

POOP TWEET

What's happening?	100
No idea for my next article! ARRGGGHHHH!	

Latest: Look out for the 2nd Issue of Poop Fiction, OUT NOW!   **Tweet**

Famous Amos
16 tweets

23	520	18
Following	Followers	Listed

Monday, 29 March

SAVED BY THE MOUNTAIN!

Thanks to Everest, I have a brilliant idea for the next issue of Poop Fiction. Mum had asked me to look after Everest. Really, it's becoming a bad habit. "Mum blogs while Amos watches Everest." So there I was using my foot to rock his cradle, when I smelt something foul. I knew that he had pooped. Beats me why babies keep doing their big business in their sleep. It's so smelly I couldn't pretend it didn't happen. As I was cleaning his backside, Mum yelled, "What does his poop look like?" Well, according to my iPhone app, it's a 3/5★. But I didn't tell her that of course.

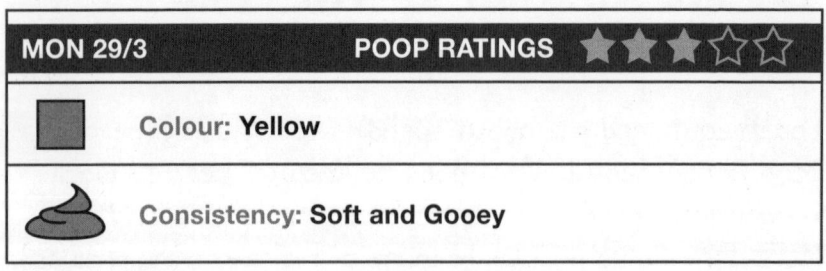

While taking a picture of the poop, an idea hit me. Maybe I could write about the uses poop has offered to mankind! Maybe not human waste, but animal poop shouldn't make anyone gag. I'm really a genius.

FEATURE #3

POOP FICTION

THE RICHNESS OF POOP

In a newspaper clipping I came across in the Straits Times, I was fascinated with the title of "Save the Earth? Answer May Lie in Sperm Whale Poop". The article shares that sperm whales help to remove the equivalent of carbon emissions from 40,000 cars each year with their faeces. How does this work? Australian biologists have found that when sperm whales defecate, they release poop in liquid form, which is rich in iron. The poop, which rises to the surface of the water, in turn stimulates the growth of phytoplankton, which traps carbon. When the phytoplankton die, the trapped carbon sinks to the deep ocean. Faecal fertilisation, which this process is called, can remove 400,000 tonnes of carbon each year. This is more than twice the amount of carbon dioxide the sperm whales release through respiration.

Wow! If sperm whale poop can do so much, what can the poop of other creatures offer?

Scientists have claimed that the study of animal faeces helps us to understand animal behaviour. We can, for example, identify the species of animals through their poop or even make an educated guess on their diet preference. Did you know that bird droppings have splotches of white in them, as they release their white and pasty urine with their poop? Or that birds eating berries can have droppings that look like sugar candy? Pink or crimson, striped with white! Err... what say we avoid eating jelly beans after reading this article?

Did you also know that carnivores, such as tigers, lions and foxes, leave behind faeces that contain hair, fur, feathers and bone? No prizes for guessing why! Duh! They pass out the undigested remains of the animals they've eaten. What about herbivores? Well, plants are difficult to digest, so lots of undigested plant parts get passed out of goats and sheep. And get this, herbivores eat almost all the time, and that means they hardly stop pooping. For cows that love to drink, their poop comes out in curdled, sloppy mounds! So do not, I repeat, do not ever step into a cow-grazing pasture.

What about something more exotic, like vampire bats? Known as desmodus rotundus, vampire bats belong to a species of bats found in South America. They feed on the blood of cattle, wild horses or chickens. Small bats the size of an adult's thumb, vampire bats will bite an animal (usually when it is sleeping) with their razor-sharp front teeth. They feed for about 20 minutes, and when they are done, the cut closes. So what do you think their poop will look like? Er.... like runny red jam, or tomato sauce? But seriously, bat poop is important because it helps to spread seeds across forests. Fruit-eating bats disperse their poop while flying in mid-air, and where their poop falls, a new plant can grow!

Apparently, some animals are like humans in cultivating practical toilet behaviour. Golden moles who live underground keep one chamber in their large burrow just for pooping. Giant otters choose an "outhouse", an area near a river bank which they will trample on to flatten the ground and poop on! Hmmm... this is like saying, "Don't poop where you eat or sleep!"

So after all this talk of poop, don't you wonder what happens to it all? Well, some creatures like millipedes make nests for their eggs out of their own poop. Some birds, like the African oven birds, build mud nests with dung of larger mammals like cattle. And of course, humans are also guilty of being just as innovative. A long time ago, houses were built using a mixture of mud and cow dung. Dung is still being burnt as fuel, in places where wood is scarce.

The homes of the Himba of Kaokoland, Africa, are simple, cone-shaped structures of saplings, bound together with palm leaves and plastered with mud and dung.

But have you ever wondered why our planet isn't overrun with poop? Well, we have the humble dung-beetle to thank. Its job is to make lunch out of poop. The dung-beetles will tunnel beneath a pile of poop, and drag it two metres underground. They eat the poop, as well as lay eggs on it. When the eggs hatch, the dung provides food for the beetle grubs. What doesn't get devoured will be buried. If seeds from fruits are passed out in poop, then new saplings will grow.

Scientists have identified 7,000 different types of dung-beetles all over the world. There are different species of dung-beetles for different types of poop. Whether it's tiny balls of rabbit faeces, leaf-laden monkey poop or splattered cow dung, the dung-beetles will take care of the job. If they can't finish the poop, worms, fungi and microbes will take over. Isn't it amazing how nature takes care of its own waste? It really gives recycling a new meaning, in using poop for food, fuel and building, and to keep life going.

And here's what you've been waiting for, the breakdown of responses we received to the questions asked in Poop Fiction #2: Do you stand or sit when you clean your bottom?

 **17** said they sit when they wipe.

 **5** said they half stand.

 **2** said they don't wipe.

Only one letter was received in answer to the Editor's question. What creative uses of toilet paper can you think of?

The reader, who calls herself Barbie's Mum, sent in pictures of a dress sewn out of toilet paper for her Barbie doll. The Editor has decided that the letter from Barbie's Mum wins ten rolls of toilet paper. Congratulations!

Finally, for an official announcement… I'm running for Tween Idol! Yes, you heard it here first. Remember to vote for me!

Meanwhile, please answer these two questions:
1. Describe the qualities you wish to see in your Tween Idol.
2. Will you vote for Amos Lee, the ingenious creator of Poop Fiction?

Write to me!

amos lee

Amos Lee for Poop Fiction

Friday, 2 April

AMOS LEE, THE TWEEN IDOL!

Wow! I received 82 letters from my supporters. They said they would vote for me as their Tween Idol! This is fantastic. But unfortunately, no one said anything about the qualities they want in their Tween Idol.

Coach had a chat with me after school. He said I shouldn't use Poop Fiction to influence voters. He called it an unfair advantage. Really? Did I even think of that? Naaaah....

Tuesday, 6 April

TWITTER CHECK

What's happening?	140		Famous Amos 18 tweets	
Latest: If you like Poop Fiction, Vote Amos for Tween Idol!!!	Tweet	35 Following	612 Followers	22 Listed

Number of followers: 612
Healthy and going up. Looking good! But I wish my mum would blog less. I find it hard to study, do research for Poop Fiction AND look after Everest.

Friday, 9 April

EVEREST THE MOUNTAIN OF TROUBLE

I have to be more careful. Just now, Everest almost swallowed my eraser! I tried putting him on my lap when I was surfing the Internet, but I didn't realise how fast he could be till he grabbed my eraser. When he put the thing in his mouth, I almost died! Mum would have fried me if Everest got the eraser down his throat. I must find a way to tie his hands without letting Mum find out.

Saturday, 10 April

WPI AND EVEREST

It's wonderful how the maternal instinct kicks in early for girls. WPI offered to watch Everest when I was doing my school work. I promised I would sign on all her T-shirts when I become the Tween Idol. I was amused to see how creative my sister was. She tricked Everest into playing "Police and Thief" in the bathroom. She had a pair of handcuffs on him while she ran around, shooting him with her water pistol. Just as well Everest was supposed to have his bath. Mum would freak out if she knew how he got wet.

Sunday, 11 April

TOM, MY CAT

Mum gave Tom away this afternoon. My kind second floor neighbour agreed to take him in. Mum said she was finding it unmanageable to look after three children and a cat. If WPI hadn't been so useful lately, I would have suggested she go instead. But better that the stray cat is gone. He will be happier with someone who has time for him. Besides, I saw Everest eating Tom's cat biscuits last night. I was too slow to stop him. This shall remain a secret between brothers. Right, Everest?

Tuesday, 13 April

CONTENDERS FOR TWEEN IDOL

I felt really hurt today. Alvin said he was running for Tween Idol. To think he is my best friend! There were three names announced by the principal. I wasn't surprised that Michael was in the lineup. But why did Alvin want to be in? I was intending to make him my campaign manager. Anthony was torn between the two of us. But when Somaly said she was helping her "boyfriend" campaign, I saw Anthony cringing. He immediately volunteered to be my campaign manager. Well, at least I have an IT whiz helping me. Hmmm... I wonder if he knows how to get on Facebook to beat Michael at his game.

Thursday, 15 April

POOP TWEET

What's happening?	22
Facebook: 500 million users!	
Twitter: 75 million users!	
Justin Bieber: 2.8 million followers!	
Amos Lee: 620 followers.	

Latest: Vote Amos for Tween Idol!   **Tweet**

Famous Amos
20 tweets

42	620	27
Following	Followers	Listed

Saturday, 17 April

MICHAEL THE COPYCAT

My campaign manager said Michael has created a Twitter account. He's tweeting about his farts. GROSS! Who's disgusting now?

Sunday, 18 April

MICHAEL'S TWEETS

I created a fake account to be Michael's follower. Sheesh... I just wanted to find out how good he is at tweeting. He's so sick I want to puke. I can't write what he's tweeting here. Yucks!

Wednesday, 21 April

MICHAEL'S GROSS TWEETS

Thursday, 22 April

POOP TWEET

What's happening? 97

Stay away from onions. Spare the goldfish!

Latest: No one wants to know about your FARTS!!!

Tweet

50 Following | 620 Followers | 27 Listed

Famous Amos
24 tweets

Sunday, 25 April

HELP! MICHAEL IS LEADING!

BAD NEWS! Anthony has been monitoring Michael's Twitter account and he has 623 followers. How did that happen? He only set up his Twitter account a few days ago!

Anthony said it wasn't surprising as with close to 600 friends on Facebook, he could easily ask them to become his Twitter followers. I need a Facebook page. Seriously and urgently!

Monday, 26 April

FACEBOOK DENIED!

Mum said no. She said it was dishonest to lie about being 13. What is she talking about? I'm going to be 13 next year! That's not lying! Women lie about being younger all the time. But men are more honest. I want to be older! What's wrong with that?

Wednesday, 28 April

YOUTUBE HERE I COME!

Anthony suggested I use YouTube to create more hype. Hmmm.... that's a good idea. I could film myself on Mum's digital camera. I need a campaign slogan. Now, what should I say? Maybe something like...

"Hi, I'm Amos Lee. I hope you will vote for me. I'm smart and creative. I must be, if I can write for Poop Fiction!"

"Your Tween Idol. The Pooplitzer Choice. Vote Amos Lee!"

I messaged Anthony my campaign slogan. He replied immediately, "Fell out of my chair. Still laughing! This takes the cake!"

What cake? And really, what's so funny about my slogan?

Friday, 30 April

CAMPAIGN ASIDE, BACK TO POOP FICTION

I've got a job to do. Research. Write. Amuse. I took less time than I did for the previous article. Practice makes perfect!

FEATURE #4

POOP FICTION

CALLING HOUSTON, WE HAVE A SERIOUS PROBLEM...

Houston. That's where America's National Aeronautics and Space Administration (NASA) Mission Control Centre is. If you remember watching movies about space exploration, the astronauts always report back to Houston to share their findings.

Everyone remembers Neil Armstrong as the first man to walk on the moon. This historical feat was achieved in 1969, on the Apollo 11. But do you know who the second man to walk on the moon is? Edwin "Buzz" Aldrin. That's how Buzz Lightyear in the Pixar film Toy Story got his name!

So what was it like to be the second man to walk on the moon? In an interview recorded for television, Buzz was quoted as saying that, "I held onto the near edge of the landing gear and checked my balance and then hesitated for a moment... I am the first person to wet his pants on the moon." Hilarious!

But seriously, with everything in space floating around, how do astronauts clean or relieve themselves? No showers are possible on board a spacecraft. But a sponge bath is manageable. When cleaning teeth, toothpaste has to be swallowed or spat into a towel. Otherwise it would float and hit you in the face! But what about using the toilet?

Well, the first step the astronaut does is to strap his thigh into a soft toilet seat which moulds to the body. Then, they have to secure their feet to the floor. After they've done their business, a pump with fans creates an air current that sucks waste away from the bottom. Called a waste collector, both male and female astronauts use it. But, every astronaut has a personal urine funnel that is attached to a collection hose. Urine and waste are treated with chemicals and dehydrated. Everything is brought back to earth to be disposed of.

Can you imagine how gross it would be, if the waste pump or urine hose broke down in space? "Calling Houston, can you send Superman up here? Please bring a vacuum cleaner and a mop." Duh!

amos lee

Amos Lee for Poop Fiction

Now for this issue's questions:
1. What has been the most embarrassing toilet moment for you?
2. Share an account of how you helped a school mate who was sick in school.

Tuesday, 4 May

MEMO FROM AMOS LEE

Dear Readers of Poop Fiction,

I apologise for asking you to submit your accounts of embarrassing toilet moments. The Editor has informed me that he's on sick leave. He got into a vomiting fit after reading 83 accounts of toilet "mis-adventures".

I thank the 83 readers who sent in your stories. But strangely, no one had anything to share about helping a sick friend in school.

Thursday, 6 May

SWIMMING OR POOP FICTION?

Coach has been really hard on me the last few weeks. He claimed that I haven't been giving my best in training. Really, what does he expect? I stay up till midnight most nights to study and do my research for Poop Fiction. If I occasionally doze off during training, I think that's pretty normal. I don't really know if I can carry on with swimming. I'm so dead tired after school. And whose idea was it to get me to write in the first place?

Saturday, 8 May

MISS WPI WANTS TO BE FAMOUS

WPI has been singing a lot lately. She's getting on my nerves. Not only does she sing badly, but Everest seems to be enjoying it too. They are always in Mum's room, WPI crooning and Everest chuckling. She calls herself a Wonder Girl now. Really, someone should teach her to be more original. But at least someone is watching Everest. Last night he rolled correction tape on his tongue. Luckily, Mum was too busy blogging to notice.

Sunday, 9 May

DIRTY LINEN ON THE BLOG

Oh man... not another embarrassing revelation about me on Mum's blog. I peeped at her laptop when she was out. She was writing about the time I was caught without toilet paper in the school toilet. Now the whole world knows that "Amos used his underwear to clean his back side, and promptly threw it away." That was actually quite a clever thing to do. But she had to add a joke.

"Good thing he didn't flush it down the toilet, like what he did one time at home. I had a hard time explaining to the plumber why my toilet was stuck with Mamy Poko Diaper Pants, size XXXL."

Yup. I was a FAT toddler. I was just being responsible by discarding my diaper pants! Why did she have to blog about it? It's private!

Wednesday, 12 May

LOUSY AT SWIMMING

I have been clocking terrible timings. Coach has been on my back, yelling and calling me names. I really think I should quit. Seeing Michael and Alvin swim so fast hurts my ego. I'm just so tired from doing so many things.

Writing. AND SWIMMING! Has he no sympathy? Isn't Poop Fiction his idea?

Friday, 14 May

POOP TWEET

Famous Amos

That's you!

Mothers just can't keep their opinions to themselves.
4:08 PM May 14th via iPhone

Best way to keep awake on the stool? Tweet! @mrslee: Throne, not stool!
4:02 PM May 14th via web

Best way to keep awake on the stool? Tweet!
3:42 PM May 14th via iPhone

Name Amos Lee
Location Singapore

80 Following **630** Followers **27** Listed

Tweets 45

Favorites

Following

Saturday, 15 May

HELLO?

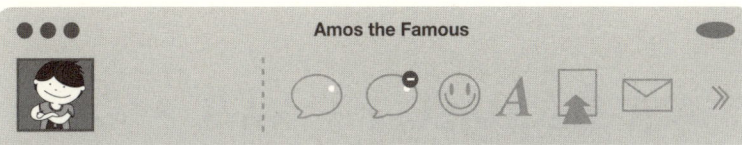

Amos the Famous
Mum? Er... I have a question. May I quit swimming?

@MrsLee
But why?

Amos the Famous
I'm too tired after studying and doing all that research for the school magazine!

@MrsLee
But you're doing very well!

Amos the Famous
That was last year.

@MrsLee
What about quitting the magazine?

Amos the Famous
NO!

@MrsLee
Why not?

Amos the Famous
It makes me popular! I have close to 1,000 followers on Twitter! They're all readers of Poop Fiction!

@MrsLee
Is it that important?

Amos the Famous
YES! I need their support! I want to be the first Tween Idol!

@MrsLee
Er... I have a comment on my blog. I need to read this. Talk to you later.

Yup. That was a conversation with my mum on IM. She's just sitting in the next room, blogging on her laptop.

Monday, 17 May

BIF AND MICHAEL. MICHAEL AND BIF.

It's official. Bif, the Goliath of the opposing school's swim team, has joined our school. And Coach has pulled him onto the relay team. Since when is there room for five? Looks like Coach wants me to go. He has been nagging me about my lack of concentration in training. Ooooohhhhh how I hate everyone! How much more can I take? I'm so tired from juggling so many duties.

Wednesday, 19 May

MISS WPI AND HER FRIEND

It's Everest's birthday today. WPI brought a friend over from school. Strange, she looks vaguely familiar. I wondered where I had seen her before. I asked her what she was doing at our place. She said she was forming a band with my sister. Pleeeuuuzz... Get real!

Friday, 21 May

THE WONDER GIRLS

Life can't possibly get worse than this. My sister is forming a girl band with her best friend! And they're calling themselves The Wonder Girls! Right. Maybe "twins" would be more like it. Someone should call up the neighbourhood police post and report them for noise pollution! Mum said I should give them a break. Look who's talking? Not only do I have to babysit when she blogs, now I have to chaperone two peaches who want to be K-Pop stars. My life is so hard!

Saturday, 22 May

WHO CALLED THE POLICE?

The police came today. They said a certain Mr Lee had called to complain about loud karaoke singing in our flat. Mum was upset. She said I had betrayed my family.

What rubbish! You mean there's no other Mr Lee among our neighbours? Anyone could have called! WPI's singing was so LOUD and AWFUL!

Sunday, 23 May

LIFE CAN GET WORSE

Yup. Mum said I must give up my room when the Wonder Girls rehearse. This is because my room faces the multi-storey car park. Sure, Mum. Empty parked cars will not call the police. I understand. But what got me really mad was when I saw Michael in my flat. He was there to pick his SISTER up! My sister, that WHINY, PESKY, IRRITATING BRAT recruited my enemy's SISTER to be her band mate! No wonder I thought she looked familiar. Good grief, they are both sooooo good-looking. I need to puke.

Monday, 24 May

RIIINNNGGGG......HELLO, ANYBODY HOME?

My mum's blogging. My sister's rehearsing with her two-girl band in my room, and my brother? He's busy chewing my pencil case. Please call back. Amos is too tired to answer the phone.

Tuesday, 25 May

NOW THEY CALL THEMSELVES "CHIPPETTES"!

Someone should teach young children that they shouldn't hanker after fame. Especially when they're totally unimaginative, and name themselves after chipmunks.

Wednesday, 26 May

POOP TWEET

Famous Amos

That's you!

ARRRGHHH!!!!
3:12 PM May 14th via iPhone

Give me a break! It's part of their song!
@mrslee: Thought it should be, "I want nobody, nobody but you!"
3:02 PM May 26th via web

Give me a break! It's part of their song!
2:48 PM May 26th via iPhone

The real Wonder Girls rocks! Nobody, nobody like you... @mrslee: Nobody, nobody like you... (likes?)
2:30 PM May 26th via web

The real Wonder Girls rocks! Nobody, nobody like you...
2:16 PM May 26th via iPhone

Name Amos Lee
Location Singapore

87 Following **640** Followers **27** Listed

Tweets 60
Favorites
Following

Friday, 28 May

AMOS TAKES ACTION

I called the Intellectual Property Office of Singapore today. The conversation went like this.

Me: I'm making a copyright infringement report

Telephone operator: If you know who you want to speak to, please press the number.

Me: I want to stop a girl band from singing. Tell me what number to press.

Telephone operator: Singing?

Me: Yes. They call themselves "The Chippettes".

Telephone operator: Can I speak to your mother?

Me: She's busy.

Telephone operator: Please call your mother.

Me: You can reach her through her blog.

Telephone operator: I'm going to hang up now. I know this is a prank call.

Me: NO! Isn't there something you can do? They are singing all the songs from Alvin and the Chipmunks! In squeaky voices! If you don't do something, I will write to the press and report you for bad service!

Telephone operator: Let's not do that. The Chippettes. Are they dressed like chipmunks?

Me: No.

Telephone operator: Are they pretending to be rats, or er... rabbits?

Me: No.

Telephone operator: So they are just humans, singing songs from Alvin and the Chipmunks.

Me: Yes.

Telephone operator: There's no copyright infringement unless they look like chipmunks, dress like chipmunks, or pretend to be rats singing like chipmunks.

That was when I hung up the phone.
And it's squirrels, not rats! Duh.

Sunday, 30 May

YOUTUBE INSPIRATION

Anthony and I have been spending a lot of time on YouTube lately. We have been watching clips to get ideas for our campaign filming.

We came across some really funny clips that I think I can use for my next issue of Poop Fiction. Great!

FEATURE #5

POOP FICTION

A FART IN BAD TASTE

Last night, I came across a YouTube clip of an elephant farting. It was so funny I fell out of my chair laughing. The camera zoomed in on the elephant's rounded rump. It released a loud phluuut! Then from a hole in the rump, an endless amount of brownish poop came pouring out! EEEKKK....! It was disgusting. It was like something Everest would do.

It's HILARIOUS to see an animal pooping!

So what is it about poop and farts that make us laugh? The worst thing that can happen to me is to fart in a lift full of people. When my sister was younger, I would pretend that it was her when I farted. But these days, she's so much faster in retaliating. She would cross two fingers and screech, "It wasn't me!" as soon as she smells one. And of course, everyone would turn to stare at me, but no one, and I repeat, no one actually believes that my mother is the culprit. Yup, with all the beans and garlic that she eats, boy, can she really fart. But being a good boy, I just grin it off.

Back to farting. I came across a book written by Jim Dawson where he mentioned the Whoopee Cushion. It's an airbag that makes rude sounds of air being squeezed through a tight, squeaky exit when some unsuspecting soul sits on it.

This smacks of a perfect prank for humiliating someone! Unfortunately, the book Did Somebody Step on a Duck? is available at the public library, which means that anyone can read about the Whoopee Cushion and create a copycat.

Last Friday during Math class, a farting game was started as a sick joke. As soon as Teacher's back was turned *(Editor's Note: All names have been deleted from this article)*, a pffffhuuutttt was heard. Everyone started to giggle. Teacher turned around and glared at me. For some reason, she thought it was me. I was baffled. I didn't do it! I shrugged and shook my head. When Teacher turned back to the board, the pffffhuuutttt became a phrroooom!

This time, I was furious. It sounded like it came from behind me. I turned and saw the culprit looking innocent, but he was grinning at me. More farts were heard, which was when Teacher went ballistic.

She screamed and said we were juvenile to play fart jokes. Well, this was pretty much what happened after that. As soon as she heard a farting sound, she would rush to the source, but when she got there, another sound would go off from the opposite end of the room. Needless to say, we had no Math lesson that day. But what really bonked me was that there was no smell at all!

Yup, that was when I realised something similar to the Whoopee Cushion was being used to send Teacher into hysterics. The entire class was put in detention that afternoon. We had to stay back after school for two hours! As punishment, we were made to write 1,000 lines of "Pffffhuuutttt or Phrroooom, I'm sorry I farted." And for every letter that was mis-spelled, we were made to re-write the entire line.

I saw the culprit with a yellow rubber duck after detention. He owned seven of them in fact. That day, he planted his friends to use the rubber ducks on Teacher. That was all the farting she heard. And to think we were all punished because of one lousy person's idea of a joke.

Amos Lee for Poop Fiction

Tuesday, 1 June

TIME FOR A BREAK

No school for a month. Hurray! I wonder what else I can do to win more followers to support me in running for Tween Idol. Anthony told me that Michael has recruited Bif to be his campaign manager. I was furious when I heard it! Where would they find time to campaign? Aren't they busy enough training for swimming?

It's different for me as Coach has put me on the reserve team. For two weeks, I've been warming the bench while Alvin, Anthony, Michael and Bif train in the relay team. I feel sooooo embarrassed. Coach even had to rub it in. He said I need to learn to think about the "greater good". Our school has a higher chance of winning competitions because Bif is a stronger swimmer than me. Well, the "greater good" in my vision happens to be winning the Tween Idol contest. And that can only happen when I gain more support from readers of Poop Fiction. So I've decided to bite the bullet. Since I'm not wanted anymore, I'll resign! This afternoon, I messaged Coach to tell him I was leaving the team.

Coach replied immediately. He said, "That's for the best. Poop Fiction is your baby. I really enjoy reading it. We will miss you!"

I'm sure I did the right thing. I have a far more important job, writing and waiting to pick up my Tween Idol trophy.

Wednesday, 2 June

HOUSTON CALLING MUM IN CYBERSPACE

Amos the Famous
Yo, Mum.

@MrsLee
Yes?

Amos the Famous
I quit swimming.

@MrsLee
You sure about that?

Amos the Famous
Ya. More time for writing.

@MrsLee
If that's what you want.

Amos the Famous
Mum, can you er... blog less?

@MrsLee
Why?

Amos the Famous
Everest is getting really difficult to watch. I don't want to be blamed if he swallows something.

@MrsLee
You're doing a great job!

Amos the Famous
Er... so you're still blogging?

@MrsLee
Yes! It's fun! Everyone's doing it! All the mums I know are on the Internet!

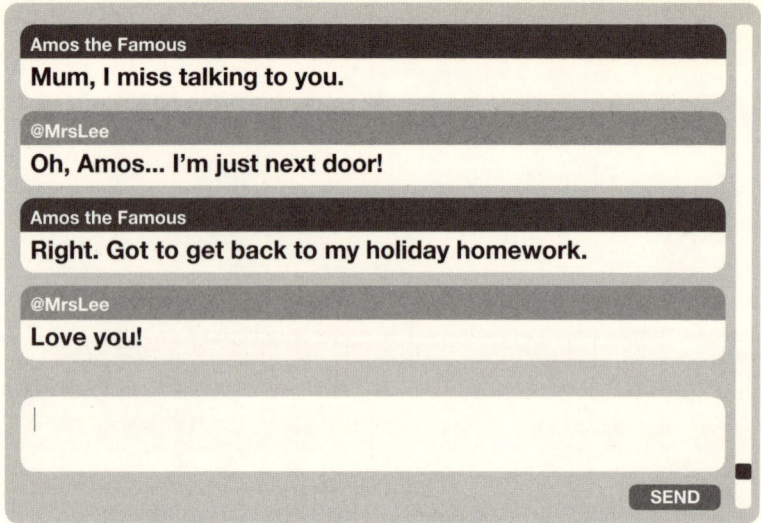

Saturday, 5 June

MISS WPI AND HER BAND

I saw a poster in school when I went back to return my library books. My sister will be putting up her first band performance after the school holidays. They're calling themselves Charice and her Band.

Wow. How exciting, a two-girl band. Maybe I should tell Mum my sister is now called Charice Lee. But someone up there must have answered my call for help. I'm really happy. So long as she doesn't pretend to be Britney and the Chippettes, the police won't be coming around again.

Thursday, 10 June

ANTHONY HARD AT WORK

Boy, my campaign manager can be really zealous. He came up with a few campaign slogans today. Here they are!

"You only vote once, but if you work it right, once is enough. Amos, Your Tween Idol!"

This is really sweet.

"It is better to light a candle than curse the darkness. Let Amos light up your life!"

What? Am I some kind of light bulb? Pleeeeeuuuzzzz.

"The Chosen Place. The Timeless People. Vote Amos. The Now."

Huh?

"You must be the change you wish to see in the world. Let Amos be your change!"

Wow! I'm inspired. I LOVE this one!

Saturday, 12 June

POOP TWEET

Famous Amos

That's you!

I'm in the toilet.
7:56 PM June 12th via iPhone

My campaign manager ought to be shot.
For plagerising! @mrslee: It's plagiarising!
Use the dictionary!"
7:53 PM June 12th via web

My campaign manager ought to be shot.
For plagerising!
7:48 PM June 12th via iPhone

You must be the change you wish to see in the world.
Let Amos be your change! @mrslee: Er, that was what
Mohandas Gandhi said. You can't use that.
7:35 PM June 12th via web

You must be the change you wish to see in the
world. Let Amos be your change!
7:22 PM June 12th via iPhone

Name Amos Lee
Location Singapore

86 **645** **34**
Following Followers Listed

Tweets 83

Favorites

Following

Sunday, 13 June

CAMPAIGN FILMING CANNED!

Oh man... my face has been so oily lately! What is wrong with me? I can fry an egg on it in the hot sun! Anthony refused to film me. He said my face looked gross on the camera. Ok, ok! That's really mean of him.

Tuesday, 15 June

ARGGHH! HELP!

It's terrible! I woke up this morning with a break out on my face. Mum said it must be something I ate. I didn't dare to go out today. Alvin came over to keep me company. I called to tell Anthony. Looks like we can't film for a looooooooooong while.

Friday, 18 June

POOP TWEET

Saturday, 19 June

VANDAL IN NEIGHBOURHOOD

Last night, Mum was surfing the Internet when she came across news of a vandal act. Pictures were posted of a masked man spraying graffiti on public mailboxes.

Such boldness! Hey, isn't vandalism punishable by law? Mum told us about an American teenager, Michael Fay, who was caught in 1994 for theft and vandalism. He was jailed for four months and caned with four strokes of the rotan. Ouch.

Sunday, 20 June

ALVIN'S CAMPAIGN

Anthony told me he saw the list of activities Somaly has planned for Alvin's campaign. He said they are all do-gooder deeds. Ooooooohhh how exciting! I can't believe Alvin has been transformed. Charity work, walkabouts in school and tree-planting. Huh? What has planting trees got to do with voting for Tween Idol? Are they for real? Next, she will have Alvin visit old folks' homes and kiss toddlers in the orphanage! Pleeeeeuuuzzzz.

Monday, 21 June

OFFICIAL NEWS REPORTS

Ahhh... the truth is out. The vandal act was merely a publicity exercise! News reports screamed, "SingPost apologises for publicity stunt" in all the newspapers. So what had been a supposed creative act of creating buzz for the Youth Olympic Games went wrong when the masked man, hired to spray-paint six mailboxes, alarmed people on the streets. Netizens were quick to take photos of the acts and post them on YouTube and several websites. However, no one was bold enough to stop the "vandal" in the act. Say, shouldn't these "citizen journalists" have spoken up? I'm sure if they had done so, the vandal would have been happy to clarify that it was only a publicity exercise.

Surely our neighbourhood would be a safer place if we were not afraid to stop the bad guys? Or we can always call the police and wait for help to arrive!

Duh. I do it all the time when there's trouble with my neighbours. The neighbourhood policemen are always eager to break up fights or question suspicious characters loitering along the corridor. Then there are also the loud karaoke singers. But for those incidents, I use my father's name when I call the police.

Friday, 25 June

WORLD CUP FEVER!

It has been two weeks into the World Cup football matches. Singapore is in the grip of football madness, and a toss between Paul and Mani.

Paul is an octopus that lives at the Sea Life Centre in Germany. Mani is a fortune-telling parakeet that lives in Little India. He's Singapore born and bred. I visited him two years ago to check if I had passed my Math exam. Now he has moved up in life to predict the future of soccer! Imagine that.

So Paul and Mani have picked cards to predict the winner of the World Cup. Paul is placing his vote on Spain. Mani, on the Netherlands. With fortune tellers like them, who needs Total Football? Forget team training, football heroes or celebrity coaches, just put your dinner money on either of these two teams. Better still, bet on both.

I wonder how accurate their prediction will be.

But if either Eight-Legs or Tweet-Tweet fail, you can always have grilled octopus or fried bird's wings for dinner.

Sunday, 27 June

A VANDAL ACT!

Why can't people learn from history? A Swiss national, Oliver Fricker, was caught trespassing and vandalising two carriages of the MRT.

Mum said Oliver Fricker's accomplice is still at large. It's sad that these vandals have to learn the hard way that they have to respect the laws of the country they're working and living in. Don't do something stupid that will get you in trouble. It's not worth the "fame".

Monday, 28 June

NOTHING BUT MUGGING!

Thanks to my acne outbreak, I didn't get to go out at all during the holidays. I have been studying at home. Yup. Mum got me to prepare for my PSLE by doing real exam papers.

I can't believe there is a market for hawking exam papers from the top schools in Singapore! Mum even had test papers delivered to our house for free.

Out of the top 20 schools' exam papers I've completed, I scored an average of 90 marks for English, Chinese, Math and Science! Well, it's not that difficult really. All the answers were attached at the back of the papers. But I only looked when I was unsure. Mum doesn't know of course. She's too busy blogging.

Holidays are over. Back to school and my favourite job – writing for Poop Fiction!

FEATURE #6

POOP FICTION

THE FART THAT WAS HEARD AROUND THE WORLD

The Editor suggested I write this article.
(Editor's note: It was my brilliant suggestion to tie in the theme of farting with the World Cup being played! Did you know that football fanatics watching TV will tolerate a roomful of farts, just to wait till half-time to go to the toilet?)

Anyway, I would like to talk about how the poor, misunderstood vuvuzela was blamed for football players missing their goals in the World Cup. Many critics have claimed that a combined force of 60,000 football fans blowing on the deafening African trumpet sounded like a herd of elephants farting! Strikers in turn claimed that they were so distracted by the loud noise, they couldn't concentrate on the match. How unfortunate. But to blame the trumpet for not being able to perform, pleeeaaassseee...! It's like whining you can't dunk your rubbish in the rubbish bin because the cars are tooting their horns too loudly.

Just what exactly is the vuvuzela? It's an air horn adapted from the kudu horn used by the African Zulu tribe. It's a cultural symbol of the African people, used in celebration with a song and dance to support sports. But really, if anyone has gone to

see a football match, since when is it ever QUIET? Fans cheer. They scream, they cry, they shout profanities that will make my mother blush; everyone makes lots of noise at the stadium! It's the whole excitement of bonding as a big spectator family, with loyalties divided for the two opposing teams.

In Singapore, we have the Kallang Wave, ripples made by spectators standing and waving their arms in continuous action. When a goal is scored, we chant, "Ole, Ole, Ole, Ole…!"

It's like we're all brothers; it's fun, and it's cool! If you ban the vuvuzela, you puncture the pride of a nation and deny it the chance to show the world how much it worships football. Isn't this missing the point of the World Cup? It's about many diversities, but one love. Football.

So back to the point of the article. (Yes, in case you haven't guessed, my Editor is crazy about football.) But he is right that the World Cup, or rather, the vuvuzela, has a co-relation with farting. Love it or hate it, you can't quell it.

To decide if it's a curse or a celebration, catch a whiff of the vuvuzela chorus on YouTube. As for me, I'm tooting for the Asian Tigers, South Korea and Japan. It doesn't matter how far they go. To qualify for the World Cup is already an inspiration to all young football players living in Asia. Ole, Ole, Ole, Ole…

Amos Lee

Amos Lee for Poop Fiction

Thursday, 1 July

GRANDMA, MY SAVIOUR

The Internet is a wonderful tool. I emailed Grandma in China for one of her recipes to get rid of acne. She replied almost immediately. I bet it's Grandpa who typed it on her behalf. I hope the recipe works.

Mum said she will go to Little India to find all the spices. Yup, in moments like this, I'm grateful the Internet has kept me connected with my grandparents, even though they are far, far away, spending their CPF retirement money holidaying!

Friday, 2 July

POOP TWEET

Saturday, 3 July

SEARCH FOR "ACNE CLEARANCE HELP"

Found many people offering homemade recipes to get rid of acne. Here are some funny ones!

Zipzit: Make a paste with oatmeal and honey. Rub into face for 20 minutes. Wash with cool water.

....

Kitchenrecipe: Place face over a bowl of hot steam for 3 minutes. Whisk 2 egg whites with 2 drops of lemon. Apply as a mask.

Wow! Imagine walking around the kitchen at night with an egg white soufflé on your face. Bet if you doze off with it, your face will be all cracked and raw in the morning heh heh...

....

This one is my favourite!

Raisinlover: Wash face with warm water. Use coarse sugar to rub over face. For acne spots, rub with a raisin. Rinse with warm water.

....

Looks like there are people all over the world suffering from acne. I'm glad I'm not alone in my misery.

Monday, 5 July

AMOS THE SPOTTED FREAK

I saw more pimples since last night. I'm really depressed. When are they going to go away? Mum warned me not to squeeze the spots. For sure I won't! They are so raw and painful! Ouuucchh!

Tuesday, 6 July

POOP TWEET

Famous Amos

That's you!

This isn't a battle of the sexes. I just wish my pimples would go away.
6:56 AM July 6th via iPhone

Research has shown that boys are TEN TIMES more likely to suffer from bad acne breakout. @grandpaElvis: But women are more likely to have it as adults! So life's fair.
6:42 AM July 6th via web

Research has shown that boys are TEN TIMES more likely to suffer from bad acne breakout.
6:32 AM July 6th via iPhone

Name Amos Lee
Location Singapore

123	648	38
Following	Followers	Listed

Tweets 96
Favorites
Following

Friday, 9 July

BATHROOM SUPPLIES

Mum must have been concerned after reading my tweets. She went out to buy an army of supplies to stock up in the bathroom.

Facial wash
(I could use this.)

Cleanser
(Huh? Why do you need to cleanse after washing? Wouldn't my face already be clean?)

Moisturiser
(Doesn't that clog up the pores again?)

Mum said I should start learning to use the stuff she bought. All of it? Wow. It will take me an hour just to get ready for school.

Monday, 12 July

FRIED BIRD BRAIN

Spain won the World Cup! Poor Mani the Bird Brain. He failed in his prediction. I dare not imagine what the football gamblers will do to him now.

Tuesday, 13 July

WPI'S DISEASE SPREAD!

Horror of horrors! This morning when Anthony called me to chat, he said I sounded really squeaky. I thought it was part of the whole acne thing, and told him I was probably coming down with a sore throat. I was just about to hang up, when he said I sounded like a chipmunk. First, pimples. Now, a chipmunk. I must be the world's biggest twit.

Wednesday, 14 July

BODY HAIR HERE, THERE, EVERYWHERE

Strange rumours are going around school. Some idiot started circulating pictures of the body hair of unsuspecting victims. It's really gross. I wonder who the fathead is.

A Primary Six girl was the first victim of the anonymous bully. Pictures of her hairy legs were circulated all over school! I recognised her. She's with Somaly on the girls' relay team. The poor thing. She's so upset she has stopped coming to school. Then, the joke got worse. The silent bully took a picture of a boy plucking armpit hair at the swimming pool. I can't decide which is more gross - the act of plucking, or that of discarding the hair into the pool.

Thursday, 15 July

WARNING DURING ASSEMBLY

Coach and the principal both spoke during assembly today. They said the recent spate of photographs being circulated in school was a serious invasion of privacy. They also said that they have classified the case as malicious bullying and will suspend the bully from school. This should stop the joke.

Everyone's so fearful of going to the swimming pool now. Training for the school team has also been suspended as Coach wants to conduct investigations.

Saturday, 17 July

MY FIRST FACIAL

Mum brought me to see her facial therapist today. She suggested I have my face properly cleansed by an expert, as my acne breakout was getting worse. It was a weird experience. I had to lie on a bed and have my face cleansed and massaged. Then the therapist squeezed out all my black heads, before placing a cooling gel on my face to reduce the swelling. When I came out of the shop, I saw a reflection of myself in the glass. I almost screamed as my pimples looked really red and angry! Mum said my face would look better in a few days' time. I sincerely hope so.

MAN TALK

Dad had a chat with me earlier. He was home early and we went out for dinner. Dad said I was going through puberty and should expect body changes. He said he had experienced it when he was my age. But hey, I bet his pimples weren't that bad! I was comforted after his talk. I felt better than I had in days!

Sunday, 18 July

PUBERTY

Did some research at the library. Dad's right. I should be expecting more changes in my body. Well, at least I found out why I sound like a chipmunk. So my vocal box is actually growing, and as my vocal chords expand, my voice will get deeper. But before that can happen, there will be false alarms like random high-pitched squeaks when I try to speak. Ha! Now I understand. I really thought WPI had passed her chipmunk disease to me! I was excited when I read about the Adam's apple. That's the bump that sticks out as the voice box protrudes from the throat.

Hmmm... why Adam? Why can't it be called Amos' apple?

Monday, 19 July

POOP TWEET

Wow! I had 26 congratulations from my male followers. Thanks bros!

Tuesday, 20 July

THE LOW-DOWN ON ACNE

Mum's advice to use facial wash and keep my face oil-free seems to have worked. Either that, or her facial therapist has voodoo power. My pimples have cleared, although the stubborn zits are still quite obvious. I've been washing my face faithfully twice a day. I even brought Mum's facial wash to school. But I have to be really discreet about using it. The last thing I want is to be caught using it! Oh… I can imagine what my enemies would say. "Amos the Tween Idol Washes His Face Like a Good Mama's Boy!"

Did more research on this horrible thing that has invaded my face. I posted an entry on Mum's blog.

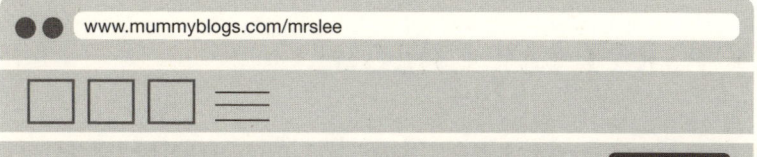

www.mummyblogs.com/mrslee

Post

Call it pimples, zits, acne, black heads or blemishes. Spots are a real pain the butt. Everyone hates them! So why do we get cursed with this "invasion"? When puberty begins, the oil glands on our head, face and elsewhere on the body become more active. Excessive oil (it has a name, sebum!) can get trapped by hair follicles and when it builds up, it forms a small blockage in the pore, which results in a "bump", or spot. These spots can appear anywhere on our face, neck, shoulder or back. So what can we do to contain this breakout?

- Keep your face clean by washing at least twice a day.
- Don't over-use harsh soaps or cleansers.
- Seek help from over-the-counter creams and facial washes. Your local pharmacy stocks a wide range of remedies like tea tree oil and antibiotic creams that will help rid acne.
- Don't be tempted to squeeze your pimples! Bacteria will set in when the skin breaks. You don't want to end up being called Moon Crater, do you?
- Get out into the sun! Sunlight (but not a tan, please) can help clear active oil glands.
- Lastly, keep your hair clean, and your fringe short! An oily fringe will surely add to your woes.

Beat the Zits by Amos Lee

Mum was very pleased with my contribution. She said she has many young mum readers suffering from acne. Really? So what my Grandpa said is true. Adults do get them, just like tweens!

Thursday, 22 July

MY FIRST PAY CHEQUE!

WOW! I got paid for my "Beat the Zits" contribution on Mum's blog! She had an offer to advertise an anti-pimple cream on her blog. Mum was generous enough to pass me the pay cheque. I'm so pleased! I made $100 for that little bit of research. I called Anthony to share the good news. He did a calculation. He claimed that at $100 an article, Coach has cheated me of $600 for six issues of Poop Fiction. Oh well, you can't get paid for everything. I told him that the publicity from the magazine has helped build my number of Twitter followers. Besides, I said it was like a form of community service, making people laugh when they have potty trouble.

Friday, 23 July

S*** MY DAD SAYS

I'm amazed at the amount of "rubbish" on the Internet. Anthony came across this successful Twitter account created by Justin Halpern, who tweets whatever his father says. Funny stuff, but almost everything is irreverent. See, I can spell! Get this, Justin's Twitter account has close to 1.46 million followers! Wow. What's even more amazing is that he has written a successful book about his relationship with his dad, and it features the best quotes from his Twitter account. The spin off from this is that a TV sitcom is going to be produced, inspired by his success!

Well, like what Coach always says, "Humour is a great laxative. But be careful what you consume, as you'll pay a heavy price in the toilet." This sounds really profound. But I can rephrase that. "Don't believe everything you read on the Internet!" The genius of Amos Lee. Simplicity in communication, duh!

Saturday, 24 July

AMOS, THE GHOST-WRITER

Mum asked me for a second contribution to her blog. This, in response to what she said were calls for help by teenage children of the mums reading her blog. Do they think she's some form of Agony Aunt? Oh for crying out loud, the truth is that she has a responsible and capable son who does her research! He even babysits her mountain of a baby boy, for FREE! Where else can you find such a sensitive and responsible big brother?

Sunday, 25 July

UNRAVELLING THE MYSTERY OF BODY HAIR

Why do teens have to face the trauma of imagining their bodies turning into werewolves? From the onset of puberty, not only do they have to deal with excessive oil glands, they have to learn to tame the mane (er, pardon the pun) on their face (thankfully for boys only), chest (er, boys only too?), armpits, arms and legs, and lastly, the unmentionable parts of the human body, the private parts.

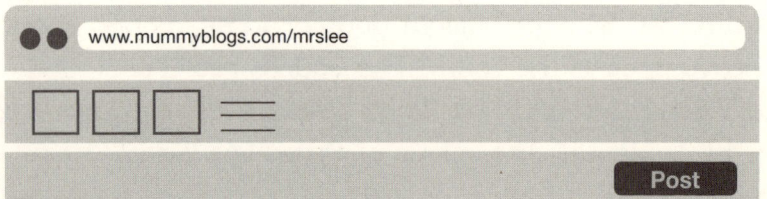

KNOW YOUR BODY HAIR

As a general rule of thumb, stay out of the moonlight when the moon is full. Then, look at your parents. If they are hairy, well, I'm sorry; this is one of the things that you will "inherit" from them too. But let's not start crying. Firstly, let's understand the purpose of body hair. It traps dirt and helps to keep you clean (the science books say that, although I find it hard to believe).

Body hair keeps you warm and protects sensitive areas. For underarm hair, it starts growing between the ages of 11 and 13. This is actually a cue to start washing under your arms everyday and maybe, start looking around to use a nice-smelling powder, or a deodorant? Other parts of the body will start growing hair when you're about 14 to 18 – your face, chest, arms and legs.

Finally, a last word. When your underarms start growing hair, you can expect the same thing to happen around your private parts. It's called pubic hair. And no, there's nothing you can do about it. Stop crying! Just keep it clean. Be warned, shave your pubic hair and it will return thicker and rougher in revenge. Don't say I didn't warn you.

Stay Home When the Moon is Full by Amos Lee

POOP TWEET

What's happening?	37
Ooooohhh, I'm so excited! Got an offer from an advertiser for a free wax service. They read Mum's blog.	

Latest: Check out my mum's blog!! mummyblogs.com/mrslee   **Tweet**

Famous Amos
99 tweets

222 Following **652** Followers **65** Listed

Monday, 26 July

NIGHTMARE ON WAX STREET

I suffered an indignity to my manhood today. Nope, I didn't try anything down below. But I was stupid enough to offer one leg for free waxing. OUCH! The horror of it! Imagine someone placing a giant piece of masking tape on your leg and ripping all the hair off! Now I know how a lizard feels like when it has its tail ripped off when fleeing a sticky trap.

I walked out of the waxing salon with one hairy leg and the other, baby-bottom smooth. What made me really mad was that my mother couldn't stop laughing on our way home. I warned her not to blog about it.

Tuesday, 27 July

ONE LEG SMOOTH

Anthony asked me today why one of my legs was looking so white and smooth. I lied that Mum experimented her home-brewed pimple busting cream on my leg. He was really excited and asked if he could try it on his forehead. Yup, Anthony has turned spotted too. He's the newest member of our Acne Club. I told him to reach Mum through her blog.

Wednesday, 28 July

ALVIN & HIS FAITHFUL CAMPAIGN MANAGER

I've always heard Mum exclaim that behind every successful man, there is a woman. Guess Alvin is just as lucky as my Dad! He has the strong and silent support of Somaly, a girl! Anthony told me that Somaly has managed to mobilise 75 old women from the Senior Citizens' Corner of Alvin's block to pledge their support for his campaign. I almost wet my trousers laughing when I heard that. Huh? What can these feeble grannies do?

Thursday, 29 July

HORROR, MY LEG ON FACEBOOK!

Alvin came over to my flat this afternoon. He showed me how I had been tagged in photos posted on Michael's Facebook page. There were two shots, one of me standing at a sink, with the focus on my waxed leg, and another, of me washing my face.

It wouldn't have been so bad, if not for the swimming cap I had on to keep my hair dry. I looked like a freak with my white leg and covered head. Oh man.... this will surely affect my followers' views of me. I was so upset I forgot to ask him what "Liang Po Po" and her gang are doing for him.

Friday, 30 July

ALVIN, MY GOOD FRIEND & RIVAL

Alvin has been trying very hard to track who took the awful photos of me for Michael's Facebook page. But he has no luck. Last night, I was at his flat till almost 10pm. He was trying his best to cheer me up. I was really grateful for his support.

When Mum came over to walk me home, we saw a bunch of old ladies at his void deck doing up posters. I was curious and went closer. I read one of their posters. It said, "Vote Alvin, He's Honest and A Pillar of Strength." Wow. I'm impressed. Look who's laughing now. Alvin can even get people who are not from school to work for him. Man, he's really good. This Tween Idol Contest is going to be a close fight.

Saturday, 31 July

BETRAYAL OF THE HIGHEST ORDER

Anthony is helping Alvin to analyse the details of my awful Facebook photos. He said they looked like they were taken in my home! Through a computer enlargement, he said he could make out the shadow of Everest in the background. Oh man... someone at home has betrayed me. I had assumed that the shots were taken in the school toilet! I think I have a pretty good idea who took the photos.

Mum said she was hurt when I asked to look through her blog. But she showed me every single post she wrote to assure me that she didn't take my photos. WPI, of course, denied it strongly too. I went through her handphone just to make sure she wasn't lying. She was sobbing when I left her in her room. She said I have abused her respect for me.

Huh? She would have been my prime suspect, if not for the fact that she has lousy skills in taking photos. When I asked Anthony next, he was angry that I had suspected him. What's WRONG with everybody? I'm only trying to find out the truth! Looks like I will never find out who the culprit is. Michael promised to take down the photos, but he refused to tell me how he got them. But he was really mean when he called me a vain idiot. I would have punched him if it hadn't been for his sister looking really scared, pleading for me to leave.

Patience. I will get my revenge. Got to get back to Poop Fiction. I have been so distracted with this Facebook incident.

FEATURE #7

POOP FICTION

TWITTER CHATTER

My mum said she enjoys reading my tweets. Well, she's just one of the hundreds of followers I have on Twitter now! What exactly makes Twitter so popular? I like it for three reasons:

1. I connect with my family on Twitter. My Grandpa and Mum reply my tweets. My Grandpa is spending time with relatives in China, while my mum is mostly too busy to talk to me; but with Twitter, they can both communicate with me as they read my thoughts and find out what I'm doing.

2. I use Twitter for spelling help. At times when I'm stuck, I send out a tweet for help. Generally, the response comes fast, with suggestions for alternative words or help to correct my spelling.

3. I enjoy reading the tweets of famous people, like Justin Bieber. I also enjoy receiving tweets from people from different parts of the world!

My mum calls Twitter the revolution of the Internet age, after Facebook. She's right. There are over 75 million users on Twitter now, and the number is still growing. Anyone, or anything, can tweet. Yup. Things. Here's an example. A tech geek found an ingenious way to engineer an office chair to "read" farts.

Anyone who farts while sitting on the chair will trigger a tweet from the computer programme that has been wired into the underside of the chair. These are some of the tweets I've seen:

"Ugh. That was a gross one."
"Someone help me!"
"Pfffffffffft!"

Not just things tweet. Even astronauts tweet! Soichi Noguchi, an astronaut from the International Space Station, has been sending astounding pictures of earth taken with TwitPics. Follow him on @Astro_Soichi!

So how else can social media empower? Consider the wide reach of Twitter in mobilising its users as citizen journalists. When the city of Mumbai in India was attacked by terrorists in 2008, the first headlines and photos that were sent out of the city under attack were made by citizens on the streets. They were ordinary people who decided to use Twitter to inform the world of what was happening in the city. I found an article, "Tweeting the Terror: How Social Media Responded to Mumbai", published by CNN, which discussed both the positive and negative impact of Twitter. You can find it through Google. This is just another example of what Twitter can do.

At a global event like the World Cup, Twitter creates a bigger impact! The official Twitter website recorded the highest number of tweets sent out per second after a goal was scored – 2,900 as compared to an average of 750 tweets per second on a normal day. It's funny to see football lovers across the globe ranting and raving about the games, their favourite players, or even lashing out at the vuvuzela. What's even funnier was reading tweets describing the ugly body parts of referees when goals were denied! *(Editor's note: all colourful words have been deleted.)*

On a commercial level, businesses have found Twitter useful to keep in touch with their customers. An example: the Albion bakery in London tweets about its products. Every time it bakes a fresh batch of bread, customers come running! Hmmm... maybe our local bakery, BreadTalk, should start BreadTweeting too.

Whatever it is, Twitter is here to stay. If astronauts, citizen journalists and even my mum (yes, she corrects my spelling when she reads my tweets) find Twitter useful, maybe there's something about it that we can all enjoy. But as my mother always says, moderation is the key to success. Just like you can't eat fried chicken wings every day, you shouldn't let social media take over your life. (Hmmm... maybe I should let my mother read this article. She's been spending tooooooo much time blogging).

On a last note, let me share that I only tweet once a day. Well, that's because I do other things when I'm tweeting. But when I tweet, I work hard at it. Trust me, it's not easy squeezing, er... characters out. And you're only allowed 140. Tweet tweet.

amos lee
Amos Lee for Poop Fiction

Monday, 2 August

LET'S GET ROLLING

Campaigning has started. We have three months to campaign before we get really busy with preparing for our PSLE. Somaly is intensifying the drive for Alvin to gain more supporters. I heard they are starting a drive to collect old newspapers to sell for money! They are raising funds for an old folks' home. Ha! Surely there must be an easier way to gather votes? I must mobilise my followers with my tweets. New media is definitely more powerful than walking the ground.

Thursday, 5 August

AMOS ON YOUTUBE

Anthony filmed a two-minute clip of me and uploaded it onto YouTube. I talked about why I should be elected Tween Idol. Anthony modified my campaign slogan. It now says, "Vote Amos! He's responsible, respectful and a role model!" Anthony filmed me rocking Everest to sleep, serving tea to my mother, and finally, typing hard on my computer writing Poop Fiction. I thought it was a brilliant clip as it showed me to be sincere and likeable. But heck, it was all for show. Mum hates tea! Besides, I don't have the patience to rock Everest to sleep. I just let him chew on my pencil case. It works every time. Just goes to show that you can never believe what you see on the Internet. But to win votes, I'll do anything.

Friday, 6 August

ALVIN, MR DO-GOODER

I can't believe it. Alvin's dad used his truck to help Alvin transport tall stacks of newspapers back to the principal's office. Wow! They had only started two days ago! To think that people actually responded to them. Anthony said Alvin and his followers visited many flats to ask for unwanted newspapers. Oh for crying out loud! He could have asked me to help. I was home all weekend, playing computer games. Sheesh... the silly boy.

I heard Alvin collected 500kg of newspapers! That's a lot of newspapers! Anthony calculated that he must have visited at least 30 households over the weekend. Wow, he's an MP in the making. Door-to-door visits, calls to help the unfortunate... Alvin is such a goooooooooood boy.

As for poor Amos, some kind of followers I have. No one watched my YouTube clip. It only registered 15 views, and they were all from me, checking to see if anyone had gone in to look at it. I'm so disappointed.

Saturday, 7 August

BIF THE UGLY BULLY

Bif has finally reared his ugly head. He had been lying low since he transferred to our school. But lately, he has been making impressive records in his swimming timings. Coach, I heard, is really pleased with his performance.

I can't say much for him as a team player in swimming, but he's been training really hard. I can't explain how I feel when I watch my friends train in swimming. Some days when I'm stressed from all the mugging, I would run down to the pool to watch Alvin and Anthony train. Then I would see the easy friendship Michael has with Bif and I get really jealous. How can former enemies become such fast friends?

Michael used to hate Bif. Bif even spat in his swimming lane once last year. But now, they are almost united in their dislike for me. Alvin said I'm imagining things. Has he gone over to the dark side too? Last week, I heard rumours circulating that Bif had been calling me a freak. "Amos, the Tween Idol freak. Mr Spotted-Face-and-Smooth-Leg."

I just ignore these rumours. The way to deal with name-calling is to ignore it. After a while, these bullies will get tired. Alvin checked Michael's Facebook. He kept his word and took my photos down.

Monday, 9 August

IT'S NATIONAL DAY!

This year, Dad managed to ballot and get NDP tickets. We got to see a FABULOUS show with floats, mass dances, aerial displays and fireworks. But the one thing that made all of us really happy was getting cool tote bags as the goodie bags. There were seven unique designs that were specially produced. All of us got to bring home a different bag. They were all really funky! We even got a board game as part of the freebies. Looking at all the merry faces, anyone would have thought that we had won the lottery.

Wednesday, 11 August

ALVIN, A TORCH BEARER

Singapore is hosting the world's first Youth Olympic Games from August 14 to 26. Alvin has been picked to be a torch bearer in the Journey of the Youth Olympic Flame which will kick off the YOG. On top of his practice runs for the event, he has also been working hard around the neighbourhood, collecting old newspapers to sell and raise money for the old folks' home. I heard he even mobilised his followers to wash the toilets in the home! Wow. How does he find time to do so many things? He is also training hard for the school's swimming relay team.

Alvin is excited about being a torch bearer. He says it's a great honour, as the torch relay will be coming from Ancient Olympia in Greece, the birthplace of the Olympic Games! Once the flame is lit, it will be transported around one city in each of the five continents - Berlin, Dakar, Mexico City, Auckland and Seoul, before being brought to Singapore! Imagine, my best friend is going to be one of 2,400 torch bearers who will carry the flame for the first time in Singapore! Oh man... this surely will help him gain more followers! Just look at the stats:

5,000 youth athletes competing in 26 sports. Team Singapore has 130 athletes competing, hurray!

500 cheer groups and 300,000 celebrants to cheer the torch bearers.

Looks like Alvin's going to gain a huge lead in the popularity contest over me. I need to gain more supporters. My only weapon is to convert my Poop Fiction readers to vote for me. What else can I do? Even YouTube has not helped!

Friday, 13 August

SWIM TEAM MEDLEY RELAY COMPETITION

This afternoon, I was sickened with jealousy. Bif led the swim team to an "inglorious" win. I witnessed him snorting and showing a loser sign at the competitors from the opposing school. He was lucky Coach didn't see what he did!

But his arrogance got the team into first position at 4:15 minutes. Coach was jumping up and down, punching his fist in the air. All the spectators cheered SOOOOOOOOO loudly for the team! Really, is it something to be proud of, putting your competitors down? Where's the spirit of sportsmanship, even if you came in first?

But I regret leaving the swim team. If I had known they would be hailed as heroes, I would have stayed on! I could have gained more supporters for my campaign.

Monday, 16 August

ALVIN AND MICHAEL LEADING THE RACE

I was right. A poll that Anthony did showed Michael leading as the Tween Idol favourite. Ratings stood at:

Michael 55%
Alvin 30%
Amos 15%

I was so horribly humiliated today. Even my sister told Alvin that she would rally her fans to vote for him. Betrayed by my own family. I hate WPI! But I have my pride. I will not beg her to help me.

Thursday, 19 August

MUM'S BLOG

I was feeling depressed today. I visited Mum's blog to take a break from homework. These days, the fastest way to get her attention is to reach her through commenting on her blog. Looks like Mum is gaining a huge following. She has so many hits on her web page! I think they average in the thousands per month!

Sunday, 22 August

I read something interesting on Mum's blog today.

www.mummyblogs.com/mrslee

PUBERTY AND WHAT YOU SHOULD KNOW

I know of many tweens who are curious about the changes their bodies are going through. Let's start with puberty. It is defined as a time when the body changes from the ages of nine through 14. This simply means that boys and girls will look more like their father and mother. Emotions will feel kind of weird. Some days you may be happy and excited, yet other days, you will feel depressed and upset. Don't worry, these are changes that your body is experiencing as you are growing up, and it's normal to have conflicting emotions.

Let's start with boys. As they grow, so do their private parts. Body hair will soon start to show, around the pubic area, at the underarms, or on legs and arms.

www.mummyblogs.com/mrslee

For girls, the same can be said. In addition, they have breasts which will start showing, and they will need to wear a bra. If you're a young girl reading this, ask your mother. She will be happy to help you pick a bra. Or speak to someone you trust, like an aunt, or a close female adult friend.

Now, girls experience something else called menstruation. What this means is that the ovaries in a girl's body have matured, and as the eggs in the ovaries are released every month into the uterus, they get something called a "period" or menstruation. It is an occasion when a small amount of blood and tissue lining the uterus gets passed out of the body. It happens once a month and lasts from a few days to a week. If you have a female pet at home like a dog or cat, you may notice that sometimes they pass out blood in their urine. It's the same process of "shedding".

It's perfectly normal!

If you have questions about your body when you don't understand the changes you see, speak to your mother, or ask your female teacher.

by Mrs Lee

Wow, I see now why Mum has a huge following on her blog. She writes about stuff that relates to young girls as well as mothers. Bet this would be useful information for someone I know. I will tell Somaly about my mum's blog.

Really, I feel inspired knowing that blogs can help people, if written responsibly and with thorough research. Mum did this on her own, without asking for my help. I should get back to writing Poop Fiction, to inspire my readers.

Thursday, 26 August

END OF YOG

Finally, the games are over! It has been a huge moment for Singapore and all of the world's youth athletes who have taken part. Singapore did well in table tennis and swimming, winning two silver medals. In archery, sailing and taekwondo, we won four bronze medals.

But what was exciting for me was to see the Under-15 National Football Team "Cubs" win a well-fought bronze medal! Last night, I was at the Jalan Besar Stadium with Dad. We saw history in the making when Singapore thrashed Montenegro 4-1 to get a foothold in the first YOG football annals. Only sportsmen can understand how badly we strive to win.

True blood, grit and sweat, we deserved it! And I almost cried when I heard 6,000 spectators bring the "lion roar" back into the field. This was what I used to hear Grandpa talk about, the magic of Singapore football in the 50s, 60s and 70s. Even World Cup fever cannot compare to the pride we experienced last night. Hmmm... maybe I should take up football in secondary school. That's one thing which Anthony, Alvin and I used to play in the void deck, before we became swimmers.

FEATURE #8

POOP FICTION

A LOOK AT THE HISTORY OF UNDERWEAR

Now that the Youth Olympic Games are over, it's back to mundane school life. Fear not, Poop Fiction is here to amuse you! We've been receiving many letters from our readers. Many have conveyed that they've enjoyed reading Poop Fiction. The biggest compliment is when some readers say that they prefer reading it to playing computer games! Awwww... thanks, that means so much to me!

My mother has been really pleased with the success of my magazine. She has suggested that I talk about underwear, seeing how topics of the unmentionables are sooooooo popular! Incidentally, she has received lots of hits on her blog. Two useful articles are "Stay Home When the Moon is Full" and "Puberty and What You Should Know". Google them on the Internet.

Back to Poop Fiction. This article presents the low-down on underwear, which I've uncovered. Let's start with diapers which all humans start their life wearing.

The earliest diapers were invented by the Native Americans. Soft moss, or even shredded bark from trees, was not spared. In India and Nepal, worn cotton saris provided relief for babies' bottoms, while in China, babies were put into trouser suits that had flaps at the crotch that could open for peeing and pooping. Cool, huh? But did you know that disposables only came into existence in the 1960s? Wow, imagine how much effort had to go into washing diapers before disposable diapers made life easier for mums.

Well, enough of baby talk. Let's move on to the boobs, er... I mean, let's trace the contours of underwear through the ages. The earliest evidence of under-wear showed that they were worn to protect the private parts.

Duh! Loincloths were worn only when people started learning how to weave cloth. Before this, breechclouts (strips of leather worn between the legs and looped over a waist-cord) were used. From the Incas to the Romans, from Africa to China, loincloths were worn in ancient history. In India, the white dhoti (a large cotton loincloth) is still worn today.

During the Middle Ages in Europe (a period before the 15th century), women wore linen outfits over their loincloths. Men wore long shirts over leggings which looked like stockings! If you have seen dramas of Shakespearean plays, you'd have noticed men in tights taking to the stage. Yup, those were real fancy leggings, but get this, they couldn't stretch! Ouch!

Knights in 15th century Europe wore special padded underwear under their body armour suits. Over in Asia, the Japanese Samurai (warriors) wore a tunic with iron scales, wide trousers and a kimono. But under all these, there was a fundoshi, which was like the loincloth. It is still being worn by sumo wrestlers today.

A discussion on women's underwear must surely include the huge, hooped petticoats which have graced the pages of fashion history. What were they? During the reign of Queen Elizabeth I of England, the "farthingale" came into fashion. It was essentially a petticoat stiffened with hoops of wood or whalebone. From hooped petticoats, women's undergarments evolved to include the "panniers" (French for "basket"), which were worn under the dress on each hip. Women back in those days preferred to be seen with tiny waists as these were considered beautiful. So they would stuff themselves into corsets which bound their waists. Over time, young girls started turning to "pantalettes", which were pants with lace or ruffles. These evolved and got shorter in length, becoming "drawers" and then "bloomers", and finally, the underpants (or "panties") that women wear today.

If you have visited a cold country before, you'd have been introduced to the "long john", which is a woollen undergarment worn to keep warm. But did you know that the "long john" owes its name to John L. Sullivan, an American boxing champion in the 1880s and 1890s? Apparently, he was famous for fighting in his long woollen underwear!

So how did the brassiere or the bra come to be invented? Well, towards the end of the 19th century, women realised that they wanted to enjoy vigorous activities, like men! Riding, dancing and playing sports—they couldn't do all these when bound by a corset! So, short, flexible "bust supporters" became more accepted, and these eventually came to be known as the brassiere, or bra for short. The first bra was patented in 1914 by Mary Phelps Jacob, a New Yorker who got her maid to sew two pieces of handkerchieves with some ribbon and cord.

And that's all I have for the long and short of underwear history!

These days, we take our underwear for granted. Whether it's underwear printed with embarrassing cartoon characters or stud briefs manufactured by designers, one thing is for sure, no one has an excuse for wearing filthy underwear. As my grandmother often says, "You never know when you will be caught with your pants down. So change your underwear everyday!"

amos lee
Amos Lee for Poop Fiction

This issue's questions:
1. What is your favourite motif for underwear?
2. How often do you change your underwear?
(I get to ask two questions as the Editor is on leave!)

Wednesday, 1 September

REPLIES FROM READERS

I received 13 letters from my readers. I'm amazed! All the girls said they are made to wear plain, white underwear by their mums while boys wear mostly blue or brown underwear. But one reader said he only wears red underwear on exam days, for luck. Hmmm.... he might as well wear it on the outside, so that he can claim to be Superman. But really, red doesn't help you to score in exams! As for how often we change our underwear, it's daily! But if you forget, you will have your mum screaming her head off, when she sniffs at it.

Friday, 3 September

MY MUM, THE CHRONIC BLOGGER

This is the waking behaviour of my mum. I actually found this posted on her blog! Oh man...

www.mummyblogs.com/mrslee

6.30am	Prepare breakfast for my two older children (bread and jam usually)
7am	Send children to school
7.30am	Blog
9am	Bathe, and then feed the baby
10am	Get baby to nap
11am	Check Facebook
12noon	Prepare lunch (anything that's quick, for example, salads or clear soups, with steamed rice)
1pm	Check Twitter, then feed baby
2pm	Pick up children from school
3pm	Surf the net while children have lunch
4pm	Take care of the laundry and ironing, and other household chores
5pm	Feed the baby
6pm	Prepare dinner (use leftovers from lunch)
7pm	Dinner with family
8pm	Check comments on Facebook, Twitter and Blog
9pm	Read to children
10pm	Last blog entry
11pm	Bedtime

I wonder if Mum needs to be counselled. Making her children eat bread and jam, salads and clear soups is a serious act of child abuse. And she should try spending less time on her laptop. SEVEN entries for blogging and social networking!

What does she have to yak about on the Internet? And with whom? Aren't the followers of her blog total strangers?

Sunday, 5 September

CHECKING OUT MUMMY BLOGS

I spent the entire afternoon snooping around Mum's blog and her links to other mums' blogs. Wow, it's a whole other universe out there - mums blogging about everything under the sun concerning their babies and children! I've read so many forum chats and blog posts. Mums are actually offering advice about mundane stuff like where to buy cheap diapers, and sharing best practices, like recipes for children's meals and how to breastfeed, with total strangers! But what's really funny are two hot topics - the best primary schools to go to and comparing the best tuition teachers in town! Cyberspace is really buzzing with these IT-savvy mums!

I calculated that on average, a stay-at-home mum can spend anything from three to seven hours on the Internet. Seven hours, that's my Mum. I think she's really overdoing it. But man... the treasure trove of information I can borrow! Wow wheee... I found things I can feature in Poop Fiction! I'm really a genius.

Monday, 6 September

MISS CHARICE AND HER BAND

Miss Charice Lee will be having a big concert during school assembly tomorrow. Mum has begged the principal for permission to film the performance. I refuse to identify with her. If anyone asks, I will say I don't know her. The embarrassment of having a squeaking singer in the family. Just my luck.

Tuesday, 7 September

A BIG BANG

Wow. I shouldn't be saying this. But I am an honest boy by nature. Miss Charice Lee can sing. There, I've said it. Either that, or the 2,000 devoted fans in my school are stone deaf and cannot differentiate between Britney the chipmunk and Charice Pempengco, the real singer with the big voice from the Philippines. WPI has been secretly watching YouTube. She has copied the singing style of the genuine Charice. That's the real star with multiple music awards that shot to fame on YouTube. And she's only 17! WPI is just a copycat.

Mum was so excited this afternoon. She posted clips of WPI singing on YouTube, and when I last checked before dinner, it already had 5,000 views. Man, the power of the Internet. It's so easy to gain a following.

Of course, I should know. Justin Bieber, my favourite pop idol, was first discovered on YouTube when he was 12! It has been four years. Justin has released a fantastic two-part album, My World and My World 2.0, and to date, My World 2.0 is ranked No. 1 on the US Billboard 200 charts. Dad bought me his CD for Christmas last year and I've been tracking his climb to fame ever since. I've also read that he will be releasing an illustrated memoir, tracking his rise to superstardom.

Wow, cool! Charice Pempengco, Justin Bieber and Miley Cyrus, also known as Hannah Montana, are the reasons why people like my sister want to be famous. They look up to the glitz and glamour of celebrity life.

But WPI forgets one thing. She may have talent, but she lacks the maturity to handle it. Surely someone who staples her skirt to raise her hemline can't be trusted with fame? I shall be a good and responsible big brother. I will tell my mother how vain my sister is. We should stop encouraging her in this ridiculous quest for fame.

Saturday, 11 September

FAME & ITS PRICE

Yup. This is becoming unbearable. I have had to deal with so many boys calling my home. Everyone is asking for Miss Charice Lee. I pretended to sound like Dad. I told them to call back when they are 20.

Wednesday, 15 September

BOO HOO HOO OVER "EVERY SINGAPOREAN SON"

I caught Mum crying over YouTube today. This, because she was watching a reality TV show of 15 army recruits going through BMT.

Mum said her Internet friends told her about the show. It's part of the Defence Ministry's attempt to let families of National Servicemen understand what basic military training is like. The YouTube programme has 18 mini episodes, each less than five minutes long. I sat down with Mum to watch the clips. They show soldiers going through field camps, clearing obstacles in the jungle and firing with their rifles. It's real, rugged and honest footage.

I asked Mum why she cried. She said, "I can't believe how short and ugly their hair cut is!" Mum, really. How shallow can you get?

Friday, 17 September

A YOUTUBE OBSESSION

Wow. Thousands are watching the clips! Imagine that. So many mums and girlfriends anxious over what their "boy-boy" is going through. Even Anthony's mum is obsessed with the "Every Singaporean Son" YouTube show.

I asked if his mum cried while watching it. He said no. But he did say she laughed when the recruits managed to break open a wild durian. She was yelling, "All grown up! Atta boy!" I asked Anthony if he watched it, he said he was too afraid to see soldiers skinning a monitor lizard for a meal. Really? I wonder who has been scaring him with incredible tales. I have heard worse ones from my Dad. He said the island, Pulau Tekong, where the soldiers are holed up, is haunted!

Oooooooooohhhhhhh..... Nine weeks on Tekong! Stay away from floating, long-haired women. Good luck, bros!

Saturday, 18 September

POOP TWEET

Famous Amos

That's you!

Maybe I meant rain cloud?
6:56 AM July 6th via iPhone

Even army boys in jungle training can gain a huge cloud. Amazing.
@mrslee: It's clout!!!!! Or do you mean cult?
6:42 AM July 6th via web

Even army boys in jungle training can gain a huge cloud. Amazing.
6:32 AM July 6th via iPhone

Name Amos Lee
Location Singapore

232	763	132
Following	Followers	Listed

Tweets   127

Favorites

Following

Tuesday, 21 September

TERRIBLE INSULT ON YOUTUBE

A YouTube clip is making its rounds. I saw it after Alvin told me about it. Michael and Bif have filmed themselves doing a snot-eating contest. Yup. How totally disgusting and immature! They pretended to blow their nose into a cup, and then took turns drinking from it. Yucks! But what's worse is seeing Michael attack me in the clip. He had an orange rubber duck which he squeezed in the background, yelling at the same time, "Fffuuuuuutttt, that's Amos farting!"

Bif added an insult, he said, "Vote for Amos, your spotted freak. He's a Fart Monitor who catches naughty children farting! Fffuuuuuutttt!"

I was so ANGRY after I saw the footage! THE HUMILIATION OF IT! I'm going to take my revenge. I will NOT take this.

Friday, 24 September

AMOS HITS BACK

I was patient and finally found my chance. I know Bif has been secretly smoking after swimming practice. I caught him once when I met Alvin behind the swimming pool. He saw us and threatened to beat us up if we told anyone. Well, I wasn't going to. But now, I will tell the whole World Wide Web! This afternoon, I trailed Bif to a spot behind the swimming pool. He didn't see me. I used my iPhone to shoot a photo of him smoking.

Later, I posted the photo on Mum's blog. I had her password to get in, as she had given it to me once. I blogged about the pitfalls of smoking, and asked if any mum had any advice for the boy caught smoking in the photo. Just as I had hoped, Anthony's mum, whom I know is an avid fan of Mum's blog, called my flat immediately. I managed to answer her call. She had recognised Bif from the photo, and asked if my mum could warn the principal. I convinced her that maybe she should do it. She agreed. I went into Mum's blog again to remove the entry on Bif. There, no trace of evidence whatsoever. Aha! Clever.

"Houston calling Bif, we have a serious problem. The principal wants to see you! Good luck!"

Tuesday, 28 September

BABY JOKES ON POOP FICTION

I can't wait for Anthony's Mum to get into action. But I need to get back to Poop Fiction. Thanks to the Mummy Bloggers!

FEATURE #9

POOP FICTION

EXTRACTS FROM A MUM'S DIARY

I have a confession. I've been too busy mugging for my tests and haven't had time to do any research on more poop-related subjects. So I took the easy way out. I checked out several blogs of mothers for inspiration! They are an incredible resource, with embarrassing stories on everything that babies and children have done. Guess which are my favourite ones? Drum roll... ta-da... potty training! Horrified? Wait till you read them! I sincerely hope you DO NOT recognise yourself in any of the entries I've found. Be scared. Be very scared.

Learn to say it properly! What were you taught?

To urinate: pee, pee-pee, tinkle, wee-wee, piss, xuuuuu?

To pass motion: defecate, poo, poo-poo, poop, doo-doo, crap, s***, let it go?

Stool: faeces (not faces), turd, ice cream, mud cake, doo-doo, big business (my personal favourite)?

To let gas out: fart, break wind, to blast off, release flatulence, to pop?

My girl learnt to pee like her brother

A mum described how she got her older son to take his 4-year-old sister to pee when she was ironing her clothes. There was silence for a while. Then she heard her son screaming, "Muuuuummmm, she just can't do it right! She's splashing all over the toilet floor!" Mum rushed over to the toilet. She was horrified to see the girl standing, with urine running down her legs.

....

From boys to men

These were verbal instructions given by a father, recorded by a mum for evidence to charge him with wrongful child conduct:
1. Remove your shorts.
2. Take aim.
3. Shoot hard at the back of the toilet seat.
4. Spray it like a cannon.
5. Jiggle the last few drops.
6. Do not flush, save water.
7. Wash your hands? Naah… that's for wimps.

I sincerely hope this was not the way you've been brought up. Please DO NOT follow the steps above. You'll give your mother a screaming fit.

....

Barbie learns to wipe

A mum found a creative way to teach her daughter the right way to wipe after big business, using a Barbie doll. She would smear peanut butter on Barbie's backside, and have the girl wipe the doll, from front to back. They practised till the mum was happy she got it right. One day after the girl had done her big business in the toilet, she yelled to her mum, "Please pass the peanut butter!"

How much paper to use?
A kid couldn't decide. He let the toilet paper roll. It rolled and rolled till the kid had to climb off the toilet seat and chase after it down the stairs.

Another kid balled up so much paper tightly in her fist that she screamed when she wiped herself.

Yet another kid tore so little paper to clean himself that he found... um, peanut butter on his hand.

....

My little soldier's target practice
A mum found a new use for her cornflakes. She dropped a few pieces of cereal into the potty and told her son, "Aim and shoot!"

....

The following was submitted by 23 angry mothers in response to the entry "From boys to men".

From mum to son:
The RIGHT potty manners!
1. Lift the toilet seat cover before peeing.
2. Keep the pee focused. Shoot ONLY into the bowl.
3. Wipe off any jiggle drops with toilet paper.
4. Discard the toilet paper and flush!
5. Wash your hands with soap.

A group of 11 mothers produced a list of pointers to use a public toilet without catching some disease.

Tips for Using a Public Toilet
1. Tear off a piece of toilet paper and use it to hold the handle/button of the flush. Flush!
2. Use toilet paper to wipe the seat cover. Discard it!
3. Remove your bottom clothing and do your business. Put your hands on your head. Don't touch anything else!
4. DO NOT scratch your nose even if it itches.
5. When you're done, clean up. Use a new piece of toilet paper to hold the handle/button of the flush. Flush!
6. Use your elbow to open the toilet door. If you are agile, step back and use your leg.
7. Wash your hands with soap.
8. Wash your hair when you reach home.

I thought this was a ridiculous list produced by a bunch of neurotic women. I showed it to Mum and she said it was brilliant!

I've been laughing so hard reading all these mums' blogs that I think I have a permanent side split. These are all priceless gems of mums' stories compiled by Amos Lee. I swear none of these stories are about me.

amos lee

Amos Lee for Poop Fiction

Friday, 1 October

IT'S MY BIRTHDAY!

Treated myself to three free birthday treats today. I visited Swensen's Restaurant in three different locations to pick up my free Firehouse ice cream. For breakfast, Mum and WPI joined me. For lunch, my best friends, Alvin, Anthony and Somaly. For dinner, it's just Dad and I. Dad said he has been very proud to hear from Mum that I'm doing very well writing for Poop Fiction. He promised to get me a laptop if I was really serious about writing. Cool! Actually, there's nothing I want more than to see someone get punished. That'll be my best birthday present ever!

Saturday, 2 October

GETTING BACK AT BIF

I heard Anthony's mum went down to school to see the principal today. Oooohhh, I wonder what they were talking about! Alvin was in school. He messaged me when he heard the principal hitting the roof and shouting loudly! Oh boy, oh boy, oh boy. This is going to be fun! Bif's going to get it for sure on Monday!

Monday, 4 October

RUMOURS IN SCHOOL

Several students heard that Bif is going to be punished for smoking. I wonder what the school will do to him.

Suspension? Nah.... too lenient. Caning? Yah... that sounds good and deserving!

Tuesday, 5 October

ME, IN TROUBLE

Well, just my luck. Anthony's mum couldn't produce any evidence of Bif smoking. Shucks! But I couldn't very well produce the photo and give myself away, could I?

I heard Coach has suspended Bif from swimming practice. That's so lame! But what I didn't bargain for was Coach asking me to take Bif's place in the relay team. There's a competition coming up and I have a bad feeling about it.

I haven't trained in months, how am I going to keep up with the team? Oh man.... Bif was supposed to be in hot soup, not me!

Monday, 11 October

URGENT SWIMMING PRACTICE

I have been training hard at the pool before and after school these few days. But because I have laid off swimming for too long, I'm not in top physical form!

I ONLY HAVE FIVE MORE DAYS TO GO BEFORE THE SWIM MEET. HOW CAN I SWIM MY BEST?

Wednesday, 13 October

RIDICULED AT PRACTICE

Michael lashed out at me when I clocked 1 minute 20 seconds for my 100m freestyle. I don't blame him as everyone averaged 58 seconds. I pulled Coach aside after practice. I told him I wished to withdraw from the competition, I said I wasn't confident of doing well. He said he had no one else to take Bif's place. Oh man... is this justice? My punishment for getting him into trouble?

Friday, 15 October

THE BIG DAY

This afternoon, I witnessed an incredibly strong school spirit in cheering for my swim team. Our competition was at the opposing school's swimming pool. I was a nervous wreck but I didn't admit it to anyone. Only Somaly guessed. She sat beside me on the bus, patting me on the shoulder occasionally. I was terrified!

Bif appeared at the pool to watch the competition. He gave me such a hateful look that I didn't dare look at him again. No one at home knew I had gone back to swimming. I didn't mention it. Only WPI knew as she had seen me training at the pool with Alvin and Anthony.

My school supporters worked their way boisterously through cheers, chanting our names as we took to the blocks. "Alvin, clap, clap, clap. Alvin!" They took turns with all our names. Alvin, Anthony, Michael and then, me.

Alvin went in first swiftly, followed by an eager Anthony. Michael was the strongest swimmer, but it was Coach's strategy to place him in third position. He wanted Michael to gain a lead for me as the fourth swimmer. But when he charged back towards me, I froze. I lost at least two seconds before he hit me on the legs. I dived in, after being rudely jarred into action. By then, the other team had recovered the advantage Michael had given me. At the last five metres, I saw Bif jumping and cheering, "Go, AMOS!" I was confused! I turned to look at him. It was my mistake. I heard the crowds cheered, "WE WON!", and then I touched the wall two seconds later. The opposing team had won.

It only took two seconds to lose the competition. The worst mistake of my life. It was all Bif's fault! Why did he have to root for me! I didn't deserve it!

What was worse was the terrible silence that greeted me when I climbed out of the pool. Alvin was close to tears. Anthony just shook his head and patted me on the back. Coach was so furious he refused to talk to me. As for Michael, he just said coldly, "So long, freak. You blew it."

As I walked past the spectators to the changing room, I heard the low murmurs of a jeer. Then it got louder and louder. By the time I hit the shower, I heard them screaming,

"BOO, AMOS, BOO!"

I can't go to school tomorrow. I am totally and absolutely destroyed. I'm more despicable than a cockroach.

Saturday, 16 October

IM WITH THE ENEMY

BIF
Yo, Freak.

Amos the Famous
Who're you calling freak? JERK!

BIF
You blew it yesterday.

Amos the Famous
You sound like a parrot, squeaking old news.

BIF
Feeling ashamed?

Amos the Famous
Why should I?

BIF
I know you squealed about me smoking in school.

Amos the Famous
It could be Alvin.

BIF
Wow. Betraying your best friend.

Amos the Famous
I'm stopping this chat.

BIF
So where were your friends when you got booed?

Amos the Famous
I have 1,000 followers behind me all the way!

BIF
Really? You mean the twits who tweet with you?

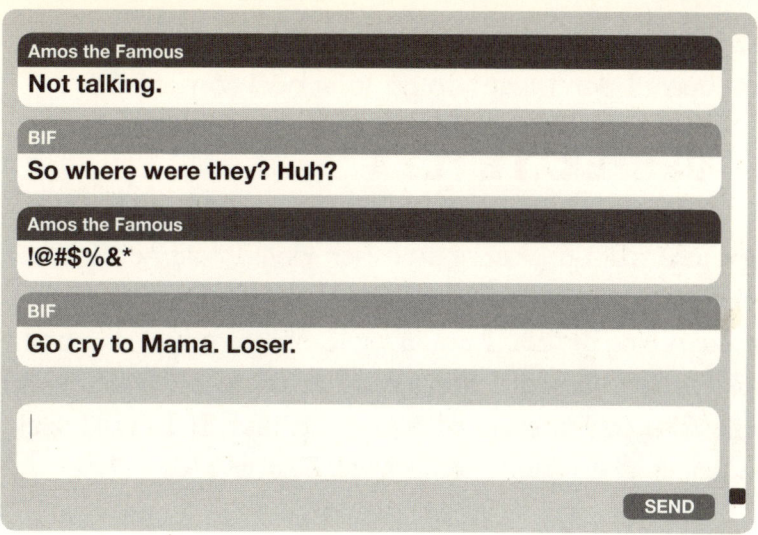

I will stop using IM. Instant Messaging is a stupid way to talk to anyone. For one, you can't punch someone you hate over the Internet. Hiding your face and calling people ugly names on the Internet is being the real loser.

Sunday, 17 October

AMOS' NEW DETERMINATION

This is it. I've decided to do something positive. I'm going to reform! This afternoon I told Mum I will take care of all the cooking in the house. Yup. Amos is turning himself into the Wonder Pot Cook! The rice cooker can cook anything!

I found lots of one pot recipes on the Internet. I asked Mum if I could stop school if I promised to work hard and become a famous chef. She laughed and said she's happy that I had volunteered to cook, but she didn't agree to let me stop school. How can she not get it?

Sunday, 17 October

(It's 10pm! I don't want to go to school tomorrow!)

MY DESPERATE PLEA

Mum was still up, checking on her blog. I told her I could make good money being a REALLY SERIOUS writer. At $100 for each blog article, I could write one article a day and still cook for the family. I don't need to go to school! She didn't agree. She said she would give me a test. If I could spell all the words she asked me to spell, I could stop school.

I spent two hours searching the Internet and looking up all the dictionaries we owned in the flat. I still couldn't find the THREE words she wanted. Man... why must she put me through this? It's almost midnight now. I'm really sleeeeeeepyy...

MUM'S SPELLING TEST

I'm no spelling bee! I'm soooooo falling asleeepppppp...

1. A mishap or embarrassing incident
   c o n t _ _ _ _ _ p s

2. A charlatan or a quack
   m _ _ n _ _ b _ _ k

3. Elegant or fine writing
   b _ l l _ s - l e _ _ _ e s

Answers from Mum:
1. contretemps   2. mountebank   3. belles-lettres

Monday, 18 October

THE FLOOD THAT SAVED MY LIFE

I told Mum this morning that I had a tummy ache and a leg sprain. She offered to call the principal to tell him I couldn't go to school. When I heard his voice booming on the other end, I suddenly panicked and told her I felt better. On the way to school, she asked if I was having problems. And that was when Amos flooded the car. It must be some magical power that mothers have over their children. The floodgates opened, and all my tears started streaming down. Mum was so alarmed with my outburst that she almost ran over a dog. After she dropped off WPI at the school gate, she drove me straight home. Phew! I promised her I would use the time to study for my PSLE.

TURNING ON THE TAP

The heavens cried buckets today too. Orchard Road was hit by massive floods! It got so bad, cars were submerged and shops along Lucky Plaza had their goods washed away. WOW! It was really scary seeing it on TV.

Mum said there were lots of jokes circulating on the Internet about floating Birkins from Hermes, the designer shop hit by floods on Orchard Road. She even said that had she known it was going to flood, she would have stood in line to grab one at a discount.

Really, what is it about women and their bags?

Tuesday, 19 October

SYMPATHY DENIED!

It poured again this morning. I worked myself up to WAIL and SOB, but thanks to WPI, I couldn't pull it off. She screamed at Mum that I had a smelly onion on me! That brat! I got stung in the eyes when she tried to grab the onion from me.

Really, someone up there should SEAL the LIPS of ALL little sisters. What's her problem? I was just trying to cut school! Mum drove me to school, and she didn't leave till she saw me walking into the assembly hall. Oh man... shrewd mums are the stuff of nightmares.

Just as I had expected, I was ostracised by everyone in school. No one spoke to me. Everyone, including my teachers, avoided looking me in the eye. But during recess, Alvin, Anthony and Somaly bought me some food. When they asked why there were tears in my eyes when I ate my prata, I told them the curry was too spicy.

WPI, on the other hand, snubbed me after school. When I saw her, I asked if we could go home together. She just looked blankly at me. She said her friends were waiting for her.

Then, she ran off with Michael's sister. When the bus came, I saw her boarding it far behind me. Alone! Michael's sister wasn't with her.

I feel terrible to have been betrayed by my own sister.

Wednesday, 20 October

EXAMS!

This is it. Everything else has to be put aside. My six years of hard work, all packed into four major exams in the next couple of days. My future depends on the results of my PSLE. I have been studying hard. Good luck, Amos!

Tuesday, 26 October

COACH'S TALK

Exams are over! Hurray!

Coach called me up today. He asked if I was serious about staying on the swim team. He said that he had spoken to the principal to let me drop writing for Poop Fiction. It was a tough call! Why must adults make life so difficult? Not only do I have to deal with a cold war in school, I have to stomach my own sister treating me like a freak! And now, this. Firstly, getting me to write for Poop Fiction was his idea, has he forgotten?

Now that Bif is out of swimming, I have to give up Poop Fiction to make up the number on the relay team.

Hey! I don't like being pushed around!

How am I going to win the Tween Idol contest if I'm not at the top of everybody's mind? Coach said if I got back to training seriously, I would be as popular as Alvin and Michael. What! Why should I follow their path? I almost told him that I wasn't quitting my writer's job. But then he said that he would take Bif if I left. That helped me to make up my mind. I told him I would stay. Anything to get back at Bif. I want to keep him off the swim team for good.

Thursday, 28 October

BIF AGAIN

I'm really down on my luck. Not only did Coach get me back to serious training, he also brought Bif back from suspension. I promised Coach I would quit my writer's job soon. Guess I will be writing my last issue of Poop Fiction.

FEATURE #10

POOP FICTION

CALLING HOUSTON, THE PARTY'S OVER!

This will be my last issue of Poop Fiction. I know, I know. I apologise for making pooping a chore from now on. Many readers have written to tell me that Poop Fiction makes going to the toilet fun. But really, you can always read other magazines while in the toilet!

Back to this issue. I'm writing about cyber-bullying. This is my story. Yes, I've been a victim.
1. I have been called terrible names on IM.
2. I have had embarrassing photos of myself put up on Facebook.
3. I have been spoofed on YouTube.

I know my bullies. If they are reading this, they know who they are too.

It's a cowardly act to use the Internet to bad-mouth someone. I have been called Mr Spotted Freak and Mr Smooth Leg. Do I deserve it? NO! I admit that I have a bad case of acne. Do you know someone who's between 9 and 12 who doesn't have pimples? Or maybe you're also experiencing it. Does calling someone else Freak, Moon Crater or Pocked-Mark Face make you feel better? Think about it. Labels hurt. They really do. The photos posted on Facebook were of me washing my face and wearing a swim cap. They were actually funny. But I didn't give permission to have them posted online. I define privacy as knowing that I can dig my nose or sniff my armpit without fear of having someone take a photo of me to put up in cyberspace. All of us have done private things that we hope no one will ever see. So why do we laugh at someone for being a hapless victim of a prank?

The next time you wear an embarrassing pair of pyjamas to bed, be very afraid that someone has taken a photo of you and posted it on Facebook. Yes, you never know when it will happen to you! Unless you choose to stop it.

Yes, YOU! If you see something online that you know is wrong, DO NOT forward it any further. If it stops with you, then you will have gone against the cyber-bully's intention of getting widespread attention. Better still, tell an adult, like your parents, or a teacher. Seek help to remove anything offensive from the site you saw. The bully victim could be someone you know, a friend, your sister, mother or somebody else's child. Please, don't be guilty of being the cyber-bully's accomplice.

We live in the age of new media. Be it blogging, using IM, "face-booking", "twittering" or sharing videos on YouTube, everything has changed in the way we communicate with people.

Although the Internet allows us to connect with distant family members or keep in touch with friends more easily, it also can hurt, exploit and intimidate. We shouldn't believe everything we see or read on the Internet. When we are faced with a cyber-bully, we should do the right thing by reporting the bully. But how do we know when we are facing one? Well, no one on the Internet should ask us to do things that are against our conscience. So if we feel uncomfortable, embarrassed, or even hurt, we should STOP all communication with the bully IMMEDIATELY! Report any act of abuse. Don't let the bully get away with it!

Now, I have a confession. I blog for my mum. Yup, I'm her ghost-writer. And I admit I can't live without my computer. I use it to chat with my friends on IM, and my grandparents on email and Twitter. I use it to look at YouTube clips to relax. When my friends come over to my flat, they let me play computer games on their Facebook accounts. Facebook is the only thing I don't have. And it's because my mum doesn't allow me to have it.

See, I do listen to my parents. They're a part of my cyber-life because I opened the door for them to get in. I have a secret to share with you too. You'll be amazed at how much less naggy parents are when they understand what we do on the Internet. Think about it. Because my mum enjoys blogging, she doesn't harp on me when I play computer games. As a trade off, I teach her how to play my favourite online games, and she follows my tweets on Twitter. We even chat on IM, when she's too busy to see me. She's like a kid herself. Funny, isn't it?

So have I learnt anything from my Internet experience? I've realised that true friends are people that you spend time with, and not those that you "meet" on the Internet. I should know. When I lost the inter-school swimming relay competition, I was jeered and ostracised. I deserved it because I hadn't tried my best. I let my school down. At that point, I thought that my hundreds of followers on Twitter would tweet me to console me. Boy, I was wrong. I didn't receive a sympathetic pat at all. Only my three true friends stood by me.

I may be quitting Poop Fiction, but I'm sticking to campaigning for Tween Idol. But I will channel my energy towards making my true friends and school proud of me. I will not use the Internet to canvas for votes.

This is Amos Lee signing out from cyberspace. Goodbye, Houston. Over and out.

amos lee
Amos Lee for Poop Fiction

Friday, 29 October

FINALLY, THE CULPRIT OWNED UP!

Something amazing happened in school today. Many students I didn't even know came up to me to shake my hand. They said that they too had been victims of cyber-bullying. Well, what do you know. Looks like my article has touched people.

But I had a bigger surprise waiting for me. I saw Michael's sister waiting for me at the bus stop. She was with WPI. She said she was sorry for having taken the two photos of me washing my face at my flat. I told her sternly not to do it again. She promised. Then something else happened. When I went up the bus, WPI grabbed my hand. She held on to me tightly as the bus moved. She even smiled at me. I allowed her to cling on to me the whole ride. Really, my sister's a klutz at taking buses. She needs something to hold on to.

Monday, 1 November

BACK TO TRAINING

Swimming has never been so difficult! I dread swimming against Bif. He has stopped calling me "freak". But he can still thrash me easily in the water. I must beat him. And I will. Even Goliath can be brought down by a stone.

Thursday, 4 November

AN EXPERIMENT

Anthony experimented with something he called a "viral campaign". He used the YouTube clip he produced of me, and posted it on... ta-da, Mummy Blogs! It was brilliant! He went into all the successful blog sites, and asked a simple question of every mum, "Do you wish your kid to be like Amos?" The last time I checked, our views had gone up to 3,200! Mums even commended me on being caring and responsible. Hey, it's a nice feeling to be told that.

Monday, 8 November

AMOS IS FAMOUS!

5,000 views today! Mum claimed that I owed my fame to her. She said two of her Internet friends recognised her in the clip and shared news of the video footage with more people. Mum, really. Two friends could rig 5,000 hits? I don't think so. I proved her wrong. When two of her so-called friends sent me an IM, I asked if they did anything to spread the footage. They said they didn't. But they asked if I would pay them if they broadcasted the footage on their blogs.

When I said I had no money, the chat ended immediately. See, you can't claim that people you meet on the Internet are your friends! Beware the danger of phantom friends with bad intentions!

Thursday, 11 November

EVEREST IN HOSPITAL

Something bad happened last night. I was so caught up with checking my YouTube hit rate that I neglected Everest. Mum wasn't watching him either. She was busy blogging. My poor brother stuffed a paper clip up his nostril. He's now in the hospital waiting for a doctor to remove the object. I can just imagine how distressed he is, and how loud he is crying! Oh, I feel so TERRIBLE!

Friday, 12 November

MUM'S QUIT BLOGGING

As the saying goes, there is always a silver lining in every cloud. Everest came home safe and sound. His nostril looked pretty inflamed, but the doctor said that the swelling would go down.

Mum cried herself hoarse. She said she would not have forgiven herself had he choked on the paper clip. Well, it was my chance to tell her that Everest had eaten cat biscuits and almost swallowed my eraser once. Her wails in response were so loud that our neighbours came to check on us. Looks like she won't be blogging anymore. Guess it's a lesson for all of us. We need to know when to stop.

No more Internet obsession! But hmmm... I wonder if I can download new games on my iPhone.

Monday, 15 November

MICHAEL AND BIF, ALVIN AND SOMALY

I saw Michael and Bif circulating flyers in school. The extent to which they will go! I can't imagine how much money Bif is putting into getting Michael to win. Is their friendship real?

Alvin, on the other hand, I heard, is making rounds with his followers at an orphanage. Really, it must be the influence of the girl beside him. He's always been such a softie, but to see him going around old folks' homes and orphanages make me realise that maybe he is serious about helping those who are less fortunate.

I've never heard him declare how much he wants to win the contest. But why is he in the running? The funny thing is that he seems to enjoy helping others. I even saw him give up his lunch box to an old man one afternoon. That, after a long day of collecting old newspapers to sell. He was obviously hungry. But he was also big-hearted.

Tuesday, 16 November

TWITTER CHECK

What's happening? 140

Latest: The paper clip has been removed from Everest's nostril.

Tweet

Famous Amos
252 tweets

513 Following 1123 Followers 831 Listed

Number of followers: 1123

I've stopped being obsessed about checking the number of followers I have. Where were they when I was at my lowest? But still, it's good for the ego to know that people are still following me.

Wednesday, 17 November

OUR SWIMMING FATE

Coach decided that we would cast ballots to choose the four swimmers for next week's inter-school relay competition. I felt sad for Anthony when he picked the shortest straw. But I was heartened when he yelled to me, "Go get them, Amos!" Yes! I've been training really hard. I'm ready for this.

Thursday, 18 November

THINGS ARE LOOKING UP

I was surprised to see that most of my acne has cleared up. I thought the facial wash Mum got me was really good, but Dad said that sunlight helped to clear the spots. Right, how could I forget! I wrote the article on how to get rid of acne.

I've also taken to lifting weights. Nothing heavy. Just light dumbbells for strength training. The good thing is that I can see my body taking shape. This is cool! I could trace a V when I looked from a certain angle in the mirror. Puberty sure helps in building body mass.

MUM'S PROTEIN SHAKE

Ground nuts, banana, egg yolk and milk powder. Gross! But it sure worked for a big toilet moment. My iPhone rated it a 5/5★! Finally!

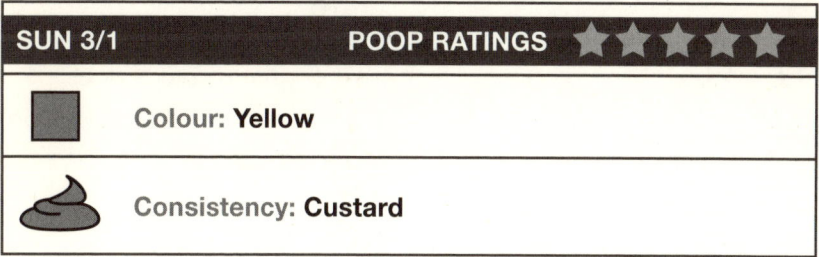

SUN 3/1	POOP RATINGS ★★★★★
■	Colour: **Yellow**
💩	Consistency: **Custard**

Oh man... Mum and her new zeal. Well, at least we're eating fewer salads now. Last night, we had a really yummy dinner. Green curry chicken and a baked yam ring. It must have taken her at least four hours to get everything together. Yup, Mum's reformed now. She has given up Internet surfing. She's still blogging, but less so though. She spends only about two hours a day on the computer. I'm really happy that she's come to her senses. For sure, Mum! We need you! Your children are more important than phantom friends on the Internet.

Friday, 19 November

THE SECOND INTER-SCHOOL RELAY COMPETITION

Today, our school beat the living daylights out of all our competitors! Before the competition, the four of us, Michael, Alvin, Bif and myself, shook hands. It was an unspoken understanding. We agreed to put aside our differences. Then we got to work.

Michael was the first to swim, followed by Alvin. The two of them couldn't catch up with the leading team. Bif went in third. He was so fast he closed the huge lead of one body length when he came back for me. This time, I didn't freeze. The last one month of serious training really helped. When I went in, we were half a body length behind the first team. I saw Bif, Michael and Alvin cheering for me on the sideline. That gave me more strength. I saw the block right ahead. Somehow, I found the energy to charge ahead and close the distance with the leading team.

It was in the last five metres that I felt a pull in my calf. I yelped and swallowed water. Then I felt myself touching the wall. Everything stood still. I felt myself going under water. Suddenly, I felt hands grabbing me. People were pulling me out of the water. I felt my chest being pumped. But my head cleared only when I saw a mouth approaching mine to breathe air. Phew! What stinky breath! It was Bif. I felt myself sputtering water. Then someone pulled me up. I could hear people screaming my name. I turned to look at the clock. I had almost drowned in the last three minutes. I'm shuddering even as I write this now.

Then, I heard the cheers. And claps. I saw people standing on their feet, stomping and yelling, "Amos. Amos. Amos!" I looked at Alvin. He grinned and hit me on the back before yelling, "We won!" I have never felt more proud of myself! I did it. I have been redeemed.

Michael and Bif held on to me as I tried to stand. The words that came out of Michael's mouth sounded ridiculous. "Nice work."

Nice? I had almost died winning the race! Surely he could have said something more generous!

Coach was very concerned about me. He drove me to the clinic to have me examined. The doctor said I had swallowed too much water, but I was fine. As we left the clinic, I almost choked on my saliva when he pumped me on the back and said, "Amos, you'd do anything to win votes, wouldn't you?"

Monday, 22 November

A SCHOOL CONCERT

My sister is really famous now. The principal had to call and ask Mum for permission to let her sing at the concert. With Mum's reformation, she has decided that fame is too much for a kid to handle. She has banned WPI from staging any further band performances. Actually, I was quite pleased. I have peace at home now. But this concert is really important. It is to celebrate the end of school, and all 3,000 students in school will get to cast their vote for their Tween Idol! I begged Mum to let WPI perform. She relented and said it will be her last performance.

Tuesday, 23 November

THOUGHTS ABOUT MY COMPETITORS

I have seen Michael change from a bully to someone I admire. I still resent him, but I look up to him for being so driven to achieve what he wants. Not only is Michael good in his studies, he also excels in sports. Every time WPI rehearses with his sister at my flat, Michael will come over to pick her up. We are enemies outside the pool, so he will be waiting at the void deck for her. But once, when I walked his sister down the stairs when it was almost night time, Michael nodded at me. Not quite a thank you, but it was close enough. At moments like those, I know he loves his sister very much.

Alvin, my best friend, has also matured. Always the charmer, he has finally admitted that he and Somaly are now officially "an item". To think that he used to be the class clown! But after winning the swimming relay last year, I can see that he's more determined to do well in his studies and sports. The last few months I have seen a compassionate side of Alvin that has made me feel very small.

I wonder who among us is really deserving of the Tween Idol title.

Wednesday, 24 November

BASTKETBALL WITH THE 3AS

I was surprised to see Alvin this afternoon. He came over to my flat and asked to play basketball. It felt like old times when we called Anthony over to join us. We used to call ourselves the 3As. We don't use that label anymore, as it seems so childish. But being together felt good.

We have grown and played together. Whatever the outcome is tomorrow, we will accept it.

Thursday, 25 November

SO WHO WILL BE TWEEN IDOL?

I have been a nervous wreck since last night. This morning, Mum hugged me before she drove off. I loved her for saying, "Win or lose, you will always be my star."

Roger, Mum!

POOP TWEET

Thursday, 25 November

END OF THE TWEEN IDOL JOURNEY

Today marked a big milestone in my life. We had a wonderful concert, led by my sister and her two-girl band. The two girls sang, "Nobody" by the Wonder Girls. They were so cute strutting and wagging their fingers at the three Tween Idols on stage. Yup, Alvin, Michael and I were serenaded by little girls, promising, "I want nobody, nobody, but you!"

After the concert, we were asked to leave the stage. But not before we had a chance to speak. This was what I said.

....

"You shouldn't vote for me because I wrote humorous stories to amuse you in the toilet. Neither should you vote for me because I almost drowned winning the swimming relay.

But you should vote for me because in the last 11 months of my life, I've learnt a great deal about myself. I have been bullied, ridiculed, jeered at, but still, I remain standing. But if what I have overcome doesn't inspire you, then I don't deserve your vote."

That was it, and then I walked off. I knew I had them when I heard my sister scream, "Amos! You have my vote!"

Friday, 26 November

FAMILY BEHIND A DEFINING MOMENT

Dad took leave and rushed home in the evening. He heard about the results and wanted to be home with me. I was really touched when Mum even skyped Grandpa in China after dinner. We had a good time chatting. I miss my grandparents so much.

At bedtime, Mum asked me if I was alright. I told her I'm a big boy, I can accept the people's choice. So who won the first Tween Idol contest? It wasn't me. I came in a close second, I lost to Alvin by 52 votes. But as a consolation, I was crowned Best Orator. However, I had the satisfaction of seeing Michael beaten soundly. He was 516 votes behind me.

I recounted the moment for Mum. Alvin went up on stage to pick up his trophy when his name was called. But he gave me a hug first. I gave him a high five, and then started chanting, "Alvin. Alvin. Alvin." The crowd picked up my line and everyone started cheering wildly when he held the trophy high above his head. By the time I told Mum

I saw Somaly crying at the back of the hall, I couldn't stop my own tears.

Mum held me tight as I cried and cried. I could sense Dad and my sister coming into the room. All of them sat beside me quietly till I fell asleep.

Saturday, 27 November

THE DAY AFTER

It was my last day in school. I went back to clear out my locker. Imagine my surprise when I saw Alvin back at "work". He went about collecting newspapers around the flats opposite our school. But what was even more amazing was to see the hundreds of followers he had with him! Alvin. The true Tween Idol. I finally understand what it takes to be one. Sincerity in inspiring excellence in others.

Sunday, 28 November

WHAT'S NEXT

We will be receiving our PSLE results next month. Mum is really anxious about my results, although she denies it. Dad said I've already done my best, and he will be happy with whichever secondary school I am posted to. I'm only worried that I won't be together with my best friends anymore.

Guess this is it. I've officially "graduated" from primary school! I have four weeks of holidays before I get my secondary school posting! Hurray!

MY LAST DIARY ENTRY

Alvin, Anthony and I got together for a swim. It felt like something we had to do to celebrate our rite of passage. As we rested by the side of the pool after 20 laps, we saw our reflection in the water. We looked hideous due to the distortion of the moonlight! Without missing a beat, the three of us howled in unison at the moon. As other swimmers stopped to look at us in alarm, we laughed and hugged one another. There and then, we knew that even if we were to part ways, we would always be looking at the same moon. Owwwwooouuul...........! We will always be brothers, FOREVER!

CNN	Cable News Network
CPF	Central Provident Fund
IM	Instant Messenger e.g. Yahoo, MSN
Liang Po Po	Grandma Liang - a popular TV character in MediaCorp Channel 8
MP	Member of Parliament
MRT	Mass Rapid Transit
NDP	National Day Parade
PSLE	Primary School Leaving Examination
YOG	Youth Olympic Games

ABOUT THE AUTHOR

Adeline Foo, a graduate student of New York University Tisch School of the Arts Asia, lives in Singapore with her husband and three children.

She is not as IT-savvy as her children. She is on Facebook and she blogs, but beyond that, she can only manage playing 'Talking Tom' and 'MissSpell' on her iPhone.

She has promised not to reveal the names of the children who provided inspiration for her stories in Poop Fiction #9, but she can be persuaded if the right price is offered.

If you've enjoyed reading this book, email her at www.amoslee.com.sg

ABOUT THE ILLUSTRATOR

Stephanie is a senior designer at Epigram, a local publishing house dedicated to producing well designed and thought-provoking books (www.epigram.com.sg).

Her first Tweet post was in 2007. She logs into Facebook daily and is currently obsessed with playing 'Pocket Frogs', 'Angry Birds' and 'Words with Friends' on her iPhone 4.

For other adorkable stuff that Stephanie has done, visit www.steffatplay.blogspot.com